Paraguay

200

YEARS OF INDEPENDENCE
IN THE HEART OF SOUTH AMERICA

Robert Munro

Commissioning Editor

A Whap production for Paraguay 200
© Robert Munro 2010

www.paraguay200.com

Publisher and Commissioning Editor: **Robert Munro**
Editorial Advisor: **Matt Holland**

Editor: **James Harrison**
Designer: **Nick Withers**

Printed by Butler Tanner & Dennis, Frome, UK

ISBN: 978-0-9567405-1-9

British Library Cataloguing-in-Publication Data

A catalogue record for this book is available from the British Library

10 9 8 7 6 5 4 3 2 1

Contents

Contributors

BENJAMIN FERNANDEZ BOGADO

Benjamin Fernandez Bogado, author, speaker, broadcaster, and university lecturer, is founder and director of Radio Libre and Fundación Libre. He has been visiting professor and speaker at numerous universities, including Harvard and Oxford. His most recent books include Á Sacudirse! *and Ý Ahora Que? See www.benjaminfernandezbogado.com*

RICHARD GOTT

Richard Gott is a writer and historian who worked for many years at the Guardian as a leader-writer and a foreign correspondent, and as the features editor. Previously a correspondent in Latin America, about which he has written extensively, he is now an honorary research fellow at the Institute for the Study of the Americas at the University of London.

MARGARET HEBBLETHWAITE

Margaret Hebblethwaite was educated at Lady Margaret Hall, Oxford, and the Gregorian University in Rome, and has written many books of theology for a general readership. From 1991 to 2000 she was Assistant Editor at the international Catholic weekly, The Tablet. *Her latest book is* Paraguay: the Bradt travel guide *published by Bradt Travel Guides Ltd UK. Margaret has lived in Santa María de Fe, Paraguay since 2000 and is the founder of a charity called the Santa Maria Education Fund. www.santamariadefe.org*

MATT HOLLAND

Matt Holland, sometime farm worker, exporter, Literature tutor, and book reviewer, is founder and Director of the Swindon Festival of Literature. He runs an educational, recreational, and cultural centre, Lower Shaw Farm, with his wife Andrea. See www.lowershawfarm.co.uk and www.swindonfestivalofliterature.co.uk He also takes poultry, poetry, and tennis seriously. Artist Leslie Holland (1907 – 2005) a number of whose lino cut illustrations appear in these pages, loved his time in Paraguay, and often said that its land, life, and people inspired some of his best work.

PETER LAMBERT

Peter Lambert is Senior Lecturer in Spanish and Latin American Studies at University of Bath. His research focuses on Paraguayan contemporary politics and society. His publications include The Transition to Democracy in Paraguay *(1998) and* The Paraguay Reader *(forthcoming), both edited with Andrew Nickson.*

ANDREA MACHAIN

Andrea Machain is a freelance broadcaster and journalist with wide experience of Paraguayan affairs. She worked for the BBC World Service in London and Miami. She now lives in Asunción and writes regularly for several journals and newspapers. She also continues her connection with the BBC contributing regularly on Paraguayan affairs.

ROBERT MUNRO

Robert Munro was born in Paraguay to a Scottish father and a Paraguayan mother. He is married to Rosemary, who plays the Paraguayan harp and they have two grown up sons and one grandson. He worked in banking in Asunción, London and New York and retired after 30 years. He now devotes his time and energy to promote Paraguay, its music, particularly the harp, and its culture. www.paraguay.org.uk

ANDREW NICKSON

Andrew Nickson is Honorary Reader in Public Management and Latin American Development at the University of Birmingham. An economist by background, he has extensive experience in Public Administration Reform in Low and Middle-Income Countries in Latin America, Sub-Saharan Africa and Asia. He has lived and worked in Paraguay and has written widely on the political and economic history and current affairs of the country. www.idd.bham.ac.uk/staff/nickson.shtml or http://works.bepress.com/andrew_nickson/

NICHOLAS REGAN

Nicholas Regan is an academic and trained classical guitarist. As a linguist he became interested in bilingualism and multilingualism in Paraguay in the 1990s, and discovered the work of Agustín Barrios while studying at the Conservatory of Music of the Universidad Católica de Asunción. He is a tutor in Applied Linguistics at the University of Birmingham and has lectured widely on the life and works of Barrios.

JOHN AND GRACIELA RENSHAW

John and Graciela Renshaw are social anthropologists. John Renshaw has a doctorate from the LSE and carried out his fieldwork in the Paraguayan Chaco. He is presently working at the Inter-American Development Bank in Washington DC. Graciela Renshaw has an MA from the University of Kent and carried out her fieldwork among the Avá-Guaraní in Eastern Paraguay. Maria Graciela Renshaw, formerly Ramirez Garcia, is an indigenous Toba Qom from Paraguay and was born in Villa del Rosario.

LUIS SZARAN

Luis Szarán is a Paraguayan musician, orchestra director, composer and musical researcher. He has directed symphonic and chamber orchestras in America and Europe. He is director of the Asunción City Symphonic Orchestra and the Phylomusica Orchestra of Asunción. He is the creator of "Sonidos de la tierra" (Sounds from the land), www.sonidosdelatierra.org.py an important community project to develop musical and cultural skills among the young of Paraguay. In 2005 Luis received the The Social Entrepreneurship Award, given by the Skoll Foundation of California (USA).

ALBERTO YANOSKY

Alberto Yanosky, scientific author, speaker, and international consultant, is Executive Director of Guyrá Paraguay, which works on biodiversity in Paraguay, and is a partner in Birdlife International. He is a specialist on conservation, population and natural ecology, wetlands ecosystems and sustainability. www.guyra.org.py

A Timeline of Paraguayan History

1811

15th May Paraguay declares independence from Spain.

First Consulate Fulgencio Yegros and Jose Gaspar Rodriguez de Francia.

1813

Dr. Jose Gaspar Rodriguez de Francia takes over government as dictator.

1840

20th September Dr. Francia dies; Second Consulate — Carlos Antonio López and Mariano Roque Alonzo.

1842

Law of the Free Womb enacted. All children of slave women are born free citizens of Paraguay.

1844

First constitution. Don Carlos Antonio López becomes first constitutional president.

1853-4

Francisco Solano López's embassy to Europe.

1858

The first British contractors arrive in Paraguay. A British firm begins constructions of a railroad, one of South America's first.

1859

U.S.A. and Paraguay sign a Friendship, Commerce and Navigation Treaty. The treaty is cited in 1998 (along with the 1963 Vienna Convention) as protecting the right of individuals jailed in a foreign land to contact their national consulate.

1862

Carlos Antonio López dies. Francisco Solano López (1826-70) assumes the Presidency following the death of his father.

1864-70

South America's War of the Triple Alliance sees Argentina, Brazil and Uruguay aligned against Paraguay. The war ends in crushing defeat of Paraguay with 90% of its adult male population killed.

1866

22nd September Battle of Curupayty (biggest victory of Paraguayan troops).

1869

5th January Asunción occupied by Triple Alliance forces.

16th August Battle of Acosta Ñu. An army composed mostly of children and old men fight 20,000 mostly Brazilian fully armed soldiers.

1870

1st March Mariscal López dies at Cerro Cora.

25th November Second Constitution.

1878

12th November American President Rutherford Hayes confirms Paraguayan sovereignty over the Chaco north of the River Pilcomayo, against Argentinian claims.

1886

A handful of German families, led by Elisabeth Nietzsche-Foerster (1935), found the Aryan colony Nueva Germania in the jungles of Paraguay (the idea originally suggested by composer Richard Wagner in 1880). The colony falls apart in 1893 and Elisabeth Nietzsche-Foerster, described by her brother, Friedrich Nietzsche (d.1900), as a "vengeful anti-Semitic goose," returns to Germany to edit and promote the work of her brother.

1887

The Centro Democratico (later Liberal Party) and the Asociacion Nacional Republicana (Colorado Party) founded.

1889

24th September Universidad Nacional de Asunción founded.

1900

Census records 635,571 inhabitants.

1904

The Liberal era begins.

1921

Sociedad Científica del Paraguay founded. Moisés S. Bertoni publishes La Civilizacion Guarani.
(see page 40)

1926

Musician Jóse Asunción Flores creates the Guarania.

1932

10th May Paraguay declares war on Bolivia (after continued occupation of the Chaco by Bolivian forces).

1932-5

The Chaco War waged between Paraguay and Bolivia over disputed territory in the Chaco Boreal. Although outnumbered and poorly equipped, the Paraguayan army win every major engagement with the Bolivians. Some 90,000 people killed.

1935

14th June A commission of neutral nations (Argentina, Brazil, Chile, Colombia, Peru, and the USA) broker an armistice in the Chaco War.
A definite settlement finally reached in 1938 awarding most of the disputed territory to Paraguay in 1938.

1939

The hero of the Chaco War, Gral Jose Felix Estigarribia elected president.

1940

Third constitution enacted during General Estigarribia's presidency. He dies just 13 months later in a plane crash. General Higinio Morínigo assumes the presidency. The Colorado Party begins its rule over Paraguay.

1945

14th February Paraguay joins the United Nations.

1954

15th August General Alfredo Stroessner (b.1912) names himself president of Paraguay following a "palace coup". This ended a 27-year chaotic period in which 22 presidents came and went.

1967

25th August Fourth Constitution (under Stroessner).

1984

5th May Itaipú Hydroelectric Dam opens.

1989

3rd February General Andres Rodriguez (d.1997 aged 73) stages coup to oust Stroessner. Some 300 people killed. In May, Andres Rodriguez is elected president and commits himself to introducing free democratic elections in 1993.

1991

26th March The Treaty of Asunción establishes the southern common market: (Mercado Común del Sur) Mercosur, between Argentina, Brazil, Paraguay and Uruguay. Later to be joined by associate members Chile (1996), Bolivia (1997), Peru (2001) and Venezuela (2004). Mexico granted observer status in 2004.

1992

20th June Fifth Constitution

1993

9th May Paraguay holds first free and democratic presidential and parliamentary elections in 50 years. Juan Carlos Wasmosy (Colorado Party) elected president.

1994

2nd September 2nd Yacyreta Hydroelectric Dam opens.

2004

1st August Ycua Bolaños Supermarket fire on the outskirts of Asunción. Over 400 people die trapped in the building. *(see page 85)*

2005

26th April Augusto Roa Bastos, one of South America's most celebrated novelists whose fictional writings often examined Paraguay's social and political struggles, dies aged 88. Bastos best known for *I, The Supreme*, a novelized version of the career of Gaspar Rodriguez de Francia, who ruled Paraguay from 1814 until 1840. *(see page 77)*

Paraguay's population reaches 6 million.

Acknowledgements

2008

20th April Paraguay elections. Fernando Lugo (56), a former Roman Catholic bishop, standing for an alliance of the Liberal and some left wing parties, defeats Blanca Ovelar, the Colorado Party candidate and a protege of outgoing President Nicanor Duarte. She sought to become Paraguay's first woman president.

15th August Fernando Lugo inaugurated as Paraguay's president — ending six decades of Colorado Party rule — a key step in the nation's democratic transformation.

2010

Paraguay's football team reaches the last eight in the 19th FIFA World Cup held in South Africa.

2011

Paraguay celebrates 200 years of Independence.

Photographs and Illustrations

Ben Cavanna
R.James Munro
Colin Munro
Marcos Esteban Alvarez
Sheila Colby
Christopher Scruby
Siew Y. Tan-Stahe
Ian Cameron Black
Henry Renshaw
Rupert Baldock
Jennifer Baldock
Leslie Holland
Wilson Park

Special thanks

Ian Cameron Black
Barry Jaggs
Peter Taylor
Maria Cristina Freeman
Diane Espinoza
Yan Speranza
Diana McClure
Rosemary Munro
Gloria Morel
Sharon McCririe

John Holland
Dennis Trott
Hectar Gatti
Jose Pedersen
Cristobal Pedersen
Arpa Roga

Elton Núñez and Tetsu Espósito www.yluux.com for the pics of Paraguayan football team supporters in Asunción 2011 for the FIFA World Cup Juanma Teixidó (p.76) http://www.flickr.com/photos/juanmateixido Michael Molinari for the Andrés Barbero museum pic (p.94) http://michelemolinari.info Javier Valdez for the picture of Berta Rojas' (p.42) www.bertarojas.com Hugo Harrison (for the map of Paraguay p.14)

MUSEO CASA DE LA INDEPENDENCIA *Robert Munro*

The colonial-style house, on the corner of Presidente Franco and 14 de Mayo, Asunción, where brave Paraguayans came out to declare the independence of the country on the night of May 14th 1811 is today a museum. It was built in 1772 by Antonio Martinez Sáenz, a Spaniard who married a Paraguayan lady: Petrona Caballero de Bazán. The walls were constructed of adobe on a bamboo and palm wood framework; with a thatched roof, now replaced by terracota tiles. The couple had two children: Pedro Pablo and Sebastián Antonio who jointly used the house with their wives: Carmen Speratti and Nicolasa Marín. Besides the two married couples, two young ladies, Facunda Speratti and Virginia Marín, sisters of Carmen and Nicolasa, also lived in the house.

A young army officer, Captain Pedro Juan Caballero, would lodge there when visiting the capital and Lieutenant Colonel Fulgencio Yegros and Lieutenant Mariano Recalde also visited the house frequently as they were courting Facunda Speratti and Virginia Marín, respectively. Across the road from the house lived Doña Juana Maria de Lara, whose nephew Lieutenant Vicente Ignacio Iturbe, lodged with her. The Martinez Sáenz's residence therefore became the perfect place to plan the conspiracy which was to rid Paraguay of colonial rule.

The house became a museum in 1965. A mural, made by the ceramist José Laterza Parodi, depicting a panoramic view Asunción in 1811, can be seen at the entrance of the museum. In 2003, businessman Nicolás Latourrette Bó generously contributed to restoring the building and donated a large number of artefacts of the period, including furniture and paintings now displayed in the museum. The same year, the Ministry of Education and Culture named Sr. Latourrette Bó "Protector of the Casa de la Independencia" and in 2005, he was declared "Life Protector" of the museum, an unprecedented honour in Paraguayan history. (It should be mentioned that Sr. Latourretee Bó's concern for the preservation of Paraguay's cultural heritage has moved him to provide financial support for the restoration and preservation of many other historical sites in Paraguay.

With thanks to Wikipedia: en.wikipedia.org/wiki/Casa_de_la_Independencia_Museum

To the eyes of the world, Paraguay — lost in the middle of South America, an island surrounded by land — has lain in lethargic slumber for over two centuries. But this heroic nation, the heart of South America, stubbornly independent, fiercely competitive, tenaciously individualistic, uniquely idiosyncratic, has faced every foe and risen to every challenge to emerge out of every crisis slightly stronger, slightly wiser, slightly prouder.

Its greatest triumph …a defeat, its greatest hero …a defeated soldier, whose final words "*Muero con mi Patria*" are on the lips and in the heart of every Paraguayan schoolchild. Paraguay always turns defeat into victory and calamity into triumph. To the gallant, generous, self-effacing people of Paraguay, this book is dedicated, in celebration of its 200 years of independence.

It is also a tribute to the original Paraguayans, whose blood runs in the veins of every person born in Paraguay. Their contribution is seldom recognised and their value often forgotten. The Paraguayan is the product of the encounter of two civilizations and the intermingling of two peoples: the European visitors and indigenous inhabitants.

In our first essay, **Peter Lambert** takes us through the formation of the Paraguayan identity. Guaranís and Spanish, Italians, Germans and Ukranians, Poles, Russians and the occasional Scot — and, more recently Japanese, Koreans and Chinese — have all combined to shape the development of national culture and society and create a strong sense of shared identity.

PROLOGUE

Next, **Richard Gott** recounts the encounter of two cultures and the contrast between them. In his article you will find sex, murder, intrigue and treachery, all the ingredients of a modern novel. **Margaret Hebblethwaite** vividly tells of that other encounter between the monotheisthic Guaranís with the Christian Gospel. Controversial to this day, the Jesuits' presence in Paraguay has left a profound and rich legacy in the nation. This essay is followed by **John and Graciela Renshaw**'s fascinating up-to-date exposé of the sad, oft forgotten story of the ancestral Paraguayans. Now few in number, with no power and little political influence in government, they cling tenaciously to their inheritance, waiting patiently for recognition, even acceptance, and for their rightful place in today's Paraguay.

In **Alberto Yanosky**'s account we discover the rich variety of the country's wildlife now precariously preserved and protected by organizations such as *Guyrá Paraguay*, and *Fundación Moisés Bertoni*.

Music has played a pivotal role in the formation of the Paraguayan ethos. **Luis Szarán** takes us through the development of this art form from the pre-colonial days to the present time.

Paraguay, *La Tierra sin Mal*, always attracted more than its fair share of community groups searching for their own utopia. At the age of six, **Matt Holland** was taken to Paraguay by his parents, who had joined one such group: the Society of Brothers, and, as he recounts, the *tierra colorada* got between his toes and into his blood. In a lively personal account, Matt recounts his childhood days and tells why he returns time and time again to the land of those formative years. **Ben Cavanna**, a professional photographer, who was born in Paraguay, returned there after 40 years and took many of the beautiful photographs in this book.

Four great names are also honoured in the book: Agustín Pío Barrios-Mangoré, by **Nicholas Regan**, now thanks to the work of John Williams truly recognised as the foremost composer of classical guitar music; Augusto Roa Bastos, by **Andrea Machain**, a writer who achieved cult status in his own lifetime; Dr. Andrés Barbero, a true polymath and the greatest philanthropist that Paraguay ever had; and Moisés Bertoni, intellectual, botanist, historian, man of letters — *el sabio Bertoni* — Swiss by birth but with a Paraguayan heart. Their fascinating lives are recounted and in them we also honour all those who came after them.

Political life in Paraguay has always been an exciting roller coaster ride. "*Freedom is a contradictory word in Paraguay*" writes **Benjamín Fernández Bogado** in the opening line of his contribution, and so is Democracy. After 35 years of dictatorship, Paraguay's incipient democracy clings precariously on the edge of a precipice. Is education the key, he asks.

Paraguay has changed out of all recognition in the two centuries since its independence and yet some deep-rooted cultural features provide an enduring link with the past. In the final chapter, **Andrew Nickson** rounds off with a frank assessment of the economic and social development of the country over its first 200 years of history. ●

Paraguay became an independent country in the early hours of 15th May, 1811 and has remained so ever since. Before that she, like the rest of South America, was a province of the superpower of the time, Spain. Influenced by the American War of Independence and the French Revolution and fuelled by a growing dislike of Spain's restrictions over economic matters, the *criollos* (locally born, of pure or mainly Spanish descent) of South America began to dream of republicanism and independence from Spain. José de San Martín in the south of the continent and Simón Bolívar in the north led the liberation movements. The turning point came when Napoleon invaded the Iberian Peninsula in 1808, considerably weakening Spain's military hold on her transatlantic colonies.

With none of the precious gold, silver or other natural resources found in much of the rest of Latin America, Paraguay lay neglected, sidetracked from the major commercial trading routes. This isolation meant few European women would venture as far as Asunción and Spanish men freely intermarried the native Guaraní women. Thus the Paraguayans became, uniquely in Latin America, a new race: the result of a mixture of the Spanish and Guaraní peoples. The Guaranís gave Paraguay not only their language but also their myths and legends, their medicine, their knowledge of fauna and flora, their favourite dishes and even perhaps their laid-back attitude.

Despite the isolation, the revolutionary ideals of independence did not pass by Paraguay, and a group of young officers and intellectuals began meeting secretly to share their dream of freedom and plan a revolution. The leader of this group was Lieutenant-Colonel Fulgencio Yegros. At 31 years of age, he had already shown his mettle at the battles of Tacuarí and Paraguarí in January 1811 — when Paraguayan troops repelled an armed invasion sent from Buenos Aires in an attempt to incorporate Paraguay into the Argentine Confederation.

On the night of 14th May 1811, the patriots heard that their plot might have been discovered. Yegros was away in the interior and in his absence a secret meeting was held at the Martinez

INTRODUCTION: THE ROAD TO INDEPENDENCE

Robert Munro

Saenz residence now known as "*la Casa de la Independencia*" *(see page 10)*. Captain Pedro Juan Caballero and Lieutenant Vicente Ignacio Iturbe (who fought with Yegros) were to be on guard duty at the barrack that night and the decision was taken to bring the coup forward. At midnight, Lieutenant Iturbe and a detachment of soldiers pulled a small canon the short distance from the barracks to the governor's house. Bernardo de Velasco y Huidobro was the governor, an experienced Spanish officer who had arrived in South America in 1803 as governor of the Guaranitic Missions. In 1806 the governership of Paraguay was added to his functions and so he became governor of the Guaranitic Missions and Paraguay.

Pointing the gun directly into the governor's bedroom window, the patriots asked Velasco to hand over power. Velasco did so and Paraguay became independent without a shot being fired and not a drop of blood shed.

With very little political experience, the patriots established a provisional government composed of the same Governor Velazco, Juan Valeriano de Zeballos, a respected Spanish citizen, and Dr. Jose Gaspar Rodriguez de Francia, who, some believe, was the brains behind the revolution, and a congress was called for 9th June 1811.

The congress decided to establish a *Junta de Gobierno,* composed of five members and chaired by Fulgencio Yegros. Its main purpose was to ensure the independence of Paraguay, not only from Spain, but also from Buenos Aires. This was secured by a treaty in which the Government of Buenos Aires recognised the independence of Paraguay and both provinces agreed to cooperate to defend their freedom. With its independence now secured, Paraguay declared itself a Republic on 12th October 1813, the first country in South America to do so.

Paraguay's heroic history as an independent nation had begun.

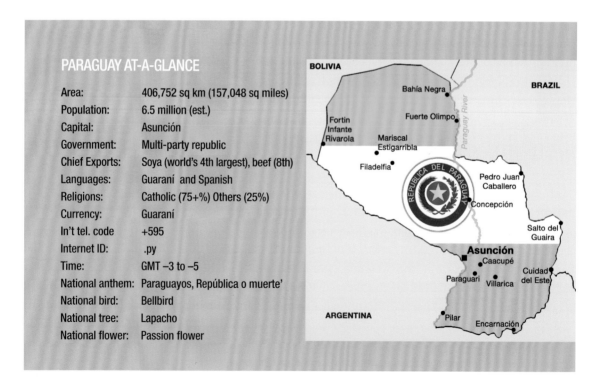

PARAGUAY AT-A-GLANCE

Area:	406,752 sq km (157,048 sq miles)
Population:	6.5 million (est.)
Capital:	Asunción
Government:	Multi-party republic
Chief Exports:	Soya (world's 4th largest), beef (8th)
Languages:	Guaraní and Spanish
Religions:	Catholic (75+%) Others (25%)
Currency:	Guaraní
In't tel. code	+595
Internet ID:	.py
Time:	GMT −3 to −5
National anthem:	Paraguayos, República o muerte'
National bird:	Bellbird
National tree:	Lapacho
National flower:	Passion flower

"**Paraguay's past does not exist as history but as legend …we do not have historians but troubadours, emotional singers of epic tales, tear-jerking guitar-playing poets of the past.**" Helio Vera (1946-2008)

A Paraguayan sociologist once suggested to me that there was no *ser nacional*, no national identity, nothing that bound Paraguayans together, other than the coincidence of a common place of birth. Nationalism, she said, had been reduced to wearing the national football shirt, waving the national flag at political demonstrations, or just populist rhetoric used by politicians in place of any ideology. On the face of it, such an analysis may appear

to have a reasonable basis. Paraguay in many ways is a nation characterized by division: rural and urban, rich and poor, Spanish and Guaraní; and Paraguayans are the result of an almost endless series of waves of immigration that make the idea of a deep-rooted Paraguayan identity highly debatable. Indeed, Paraguay, like many nations, is perhaps as much divided along grounds of language, race, class and gender as it is united. And yet …there exists an undeniably strong sense of shared identity among Paraguayans based not on any aggressive sense of nationalism but rather on a shared outlook on the world shaped by certain defining influences and experiences of Paraguayan history and culture.

HISTORY, IDENTITY AND PARAGUAYIDAD

Peter Lambert

History and nationalism

The search for national identity is not new, and runs through much of the writing, academic or not, on Paraguayan history. Yet although opinions on history abound, the absence of major objective works on the history of Paraguay is striking, and is a reflection of a deep lack of consensus regarding fundamental historical events. This of course makes the themes of Paraguayan history (and any understanding of her national identity) an extraordinarily contested field — or minefield. So we have Helio Vera's pertinent quote at the top of this article. A prominent Paraguayan sociologist, his remark tells us that the writing (and rewriting) of history by such 'troubadours' of national identity, and the confusion between myth and reality, history and fable, are a long established tradition.

From 1870 until the Chaco War of 1932–5 the idea of the nation had been dominated by the liberal view as promoted by writers such as Cecilio Báez (also Pargauay's 18th President for less than a year) that Spanish colonial rule was replaced by republican despotism under the dictators Dr. Francia (who ruled from 1814–40) and his successor Carlos Antonio López (1840–62). A highly centralized authoritarian state had frustrated the liberal ideas of liberty, free trade and international integration, so the story went, and Paraguay had become the 'China of the Americas'

— closed, authoritarian, and characterized by a lack of scientific, cultural and political enlightenment. Those who resisted this 'official' version felt it was a history imposed by the victors of the Triple Alliance War — Argentina, Brazil and Uruguay — who also occupied Paraguay following the bloodiest conflict in Latin American history (1864–70).

This version was challenged in the first decades of the 20th century by a new interpretation, developed by a group of writers among the so-called Generation of 900. Through an intentionally rousing and poetic literature, writers such as Juan E. O'Leary (1879–1968), J. Natalicio González (1896–1966) and Manuel Dominguez (1869–1935) attacked the old stories and created a new historical narrative, which sought to restore a sense of national pride, identity and direction to a nation devastated by war.

This new nationalism was based on a number of disputed but emotionally powerful tenets, which turned the liberal version on its head. The Nationalist Period (1814–70) was reinterpreted not as one of authoritarian despotism, but of independent development, progress and prosperity — a veritable 'golden age', led by the 'father' of the nation, Dr. Francia and the 'builder of the nation', Carlos Antonio López. Most strikingly, Francisco Solano López, was transformed from his previous vilification as an evil, and perhaps mad, tyrant who had led Paraguay to disaster in the Triple Alliance War, to the human representation of the nation, the essence of *paraguayidad*. Parallel to this, the catastrophe of the Triple Alliance War was transformed into an heroic defense and inevitable but glorious defeat, complete with landscapes (the ruins of Humaitá) symbols (the tragic battlefields of Acosta Ñu) and heroes (Caballero, Díaz and of course, López).

Nationalist writers also developed the idea of the *raza guaraní*, a founding myth of common ancestry and of common ethnic community. Paraguayans, it was argued, were the result of the mix of Spanish and Guaraní, the enlightened European and the noble savage, the 'warrior farmer'. This formed the basis for the claim of a unique and distinctive nation in terms of history, culture, land and race. By the mid-1930s , this glorified narrative of the Paraguayan nation had become part of the official government line. Most importantly, following the Civil War of 1947, it provided the ideological foundations of the Colorado Party and the subsequent three-decade rule of General Alfredo Stroessner — among the last of the old-style military dictators. These deep and emotionally-charged differences in the basic interpretation of Paraguay's recent past remain alive today, and help explain why so few historians (quite understandably) choose to write on Paraguayan history. But if Paraguay's official nationalist story is considered tainted (because it is too closely linked to the Stroessner dictatorship for comfort), and Paraguayans remain divided over the interpretation of its history and identity, what is left? What then are the ties that bind Paraguay?

The Myth of the *Raza Guaraní*

Before examining the factors that may bind Paraguayans, it is important to address the myth of the *raza guaraní* especially in relation to the false image presented — often by foreign journalists — of Paraguay as a country with a large indigenous (Guaraní) population. In fact, Paraguay's indigenous population is today very small (less than 3% of the population) and it is not Guaraní (which is more a linguistic than cultural or racial term). Even when the Spanish arrived, Guaraní-speaking groups were only present in parts of the East, while an array of very different groups (in terms of language and culture) dominated other areas.

Paraguay is actually largely *mestizo*. This is a result of the Spanish colonial policy of encouraging inter-marriage, or at least inter-breeding, and equally importantly the successful, innovative and unique effort by Dr Francia to destroy the power of the Spanish (and hence the white ruling class) following independence, by obliging white Spaniards to marry *mestizos* or indigenous people. Any remaining concept of a Paraguayan 'race' was further diluted by the annihilation caused by the Triple Alliance War which decimated up to 90% of the adult male population, and led to a sustained period of repopulation fuelled partly by immigration. Many Paraguayans may passionately believe themselves to be part of a Guaraní 'race', but genetically any 'Guaraní blood' is likely to be very thinly dispersed in modern Paraguay. As anthropologist and Guaraní researcher Bartomeu Melià has argued, "*given the historic and social reality of Paraguay and the fusion of such diverse ethnic elements — above all European — the concept of race has no meaning at all. The so-called Guaraní race is in no way a defining element of our national being.*"

Defining Paraguay

So if it is not race, then what does define Paraguay in terms of identity? There are perhaps five factors that have influenced Paraguay's historical development and identity through shared national experience: isolation, war, land, immigration, and language.

Isolation: Landlocked, far from major commercial trading routes, with none of the gold, silver or other natural resources coveted in much of the rest of Latin America, Paraguay languished as a backwater during most of the colonial period. As Buenos Aires, Lima, Montevideo and Santiago grew, so Asunción was neglected, cut off from the west by the vast inhospitable Chaco semi-desert and from the sea by Brazil and Buenos Aires (which controlled its only trade route, the River Paraná). This geographical isolation was intensified under Dr Francia who, facing the threat of annexation from both Argentina and Brazil and wisely distrustful of British intentions, placed strict controls on international trade and contact.

Self-imposed isolation, coupled with authoritarian rule added to the reality and the perception of Paraguay as an isolated, mainly Guaraní-speaking oddity, the 'island surrounded by land'. That was until the catastrophe of the Triple Alliance War brought it back into line. However, isolation did not stop when that war ended in 1870, but continued to be a recurrent theme in Paraguayan history, exaggerating concepts of difference and at times used for political convenience. The highly successful policy of 'benign isolation', as Paraguayan economist Fernando Masi has termed it, was adopted by the Stroessner dictatorship as a means of continuing constructive relations with key partners (most notably the United States) while allowing Paraguay to keep out of the international limelight and avoid political condemnation for human rights abuses. Out of sight, out of mind. Paraguay returned to its position as the oft forgotten land, a fruitful source of fiction, rumour and fable.

Such isolation had a huge cultural impact, creating a more inward-looking society and fostering a stronger sense of shared cultural norms and identity, something that, in an increasingly homogenised and globalized world, certainly had its advantages.

War: Isolation has been heightened by the intimately related factor of internal power politics and warfare. Whilst until recently Paraguay was effectively isolated from Bolivia to the north due to the inhospitable nature

IMAGES OF PARAGUAY TODAY

The ever-present horse as transport and Paraguayan horsemanship, National Pantheon of The Heroes, Asunción and the abundance of flower and fruit markets.

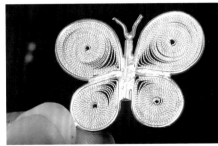

IMAGES OF PARAGUAY TODAY

Asado a la Estaca, fine filigree jewellery crafts, the ever-popular chipa and a seller with *canasto de chipa*, the Pink Lapacho tree, Asuncíon's cathedral, and the rise and rise of Paraguayan harp playing.

of the Gran Chaco, its history has been dominated by the overbearing presence of its two other neighbours, Brazil and Argentina. Even today, Paraguay's population of six million is dwarfed by Brazil's population of 192 million. The harsh realities of politics have reflected this imbalance in power, resources, and population, in any number of ways, ranging from the almost perpetual post-colonial fear of Argentinian or Brazilian annexation, to the historical issue of gaining permission from Buenos Aires to have access to the sea, to Paraguay's present efforts to rectify what it sees as the scandalously unfair financial terms of the 1973 treaty concerning the joint Itaipú hydroelectric project with Brazil. A history of living between two regional giants has shaped a certain shared perception of the world and Paraguay's place within it.

This perception has been further affected by the experience of Paraguay's essentially defensive international wars with all of its neighbours. Indeed, from independence Paraguay found its very existence threatened by its neighbours. It defended itself successfully against General Belgano's 'army of liberation' sent from Buenos Aires in 1811. It also went to war with Bolivia in the brutal and tragic Chaco War (1932-35) against what it saw as a creeping Bolivian invasion of disputed territory. However, it could do little against the combined forces of Brazil, Argentina and Uruguay in the infamous Triple Alliance War (1864-70). Whether one believes this to be a heroic defence by the entire Paraguayan nation (women and children included) against an international alliance bent on destroying the country, or the result of the exaggerated political ambitions of an arrogant dictator, Francisco Solano López, the very real fear of imminent destruction and possible elimination as a sovereign people led Paraguayans to fight to the bitter end. The magnitude of the destruction was extraordinary; as well as losing 25% of its territory to Brazil and Argentina (including the Iguazú Falls) it also lost over 60% of its total population. Such sacrifice and devastation scarred the collective memory, whilst the shared suffering and the collective sense of irreparable injustice proved fertile ground for a strong sense of national identity, solidarity and difference.

Immigration: If the concept of the *raza guaraní* is highly questionable in genetic terms, (however much it is 'felt' or referred to by many Paraguayans), what is the ethnic composition of Paraguay? In what was intended as an antidote to any idea of racial nationalism, Helio Vera (again quoted) attempted to summarize the 'ingredients' of a Paraguayan in his tongue-in-cheek '*Dona Petrona's Recipe*'; To make a Paraguayan...

> "*Put six measures of indigenous, mainly Guaraní from the central region, without overlooking a little Payaguá, Guayaquí, Guaikuru, Tobá, Moró or Chamacoco. Add two parts of Andalucian and Extremeño and a little Basque. Stir in a pinch of English, German and Italian, as well as North African or Jewish of unknown origin. Do not forget to add a generous helping of black African.*
>
> *Be patient and wait a couple of centuries before adding one equal measure of Italian and German. Wait a little longer and sprinkle in some Arab, French, Croat, Serb, Montenegrin, Polish, Russian and Ukrainian. Stir well. Do not rush because you will also need to add some Armenian, Scandinavian and Irish. Pause and breathe deeply to gather your energy. However, do not be tempted to think you have finished because, before taking the cake out of the oven, you will need to add equally generous portions of Japanese, Chinese and Korean.*"

Of course, what Vera alludes to is the fact that to a great extent Paraguay is a country of immigrants. Isolationism did not stop waves of immigration, most notably from Europe, but also from neighbouring countries.

Paradoxically, many immigrants were attracted by the very image of Paraguay as an isolated backwater, of starting afresh in 'the land without evil', an image that inspired attempts to set up a multitude of new colonies, some idealistic (*Nueva Australia*), some religious (the Mennonites who developed areas of the Chaco), and some more sinister (*Nueva Germania*). Either way, Paraguay was seen from the outside as a new Eden, the land for new beginnings.

This is relevant to the question of identity for two reasons: first, it reflects the openness of Paraguayans (who are famously welcoming) to foreigners, dispelling any myth of xenophobia resulting from isolation. Racism towards foreigners is almost non-existent and contrasts markedly to such problems in Western Europe, for example (although the significant recent growth in the *brasiguayo* population and the related expansion of soya production are certainly increasing social tensions and threatening such tolerance). Second, the cultural impact of immigration is reflected in a variety of ways: from the Spanish spoken in Paraguay, which has been nuanced by regional (Portuguese) as well as European (especially Italian) influences, to the flora (even the ubiquitous mango, Paraguayan Jasmine and sugarcane are essentially imports), to music (the harp, the polka), to popular cuisine (pasta, hamburgers and rice). While this might further undermine the idea of a 'Guaraní' identity, it should not be be equated with a lack of national identity. In many ways, quite the reverse is true.

Language: Given that immigration has played such an important role in the development of a former Spanish colony, and that indigenous peoples make up so few of the population, it is perhaps striking to an outsider that Guaraní is a key defining characteristic in terms of language. Despite 300 years of Spanish rule, everyone spoke in Guaraní at least until the beginning of the 20th century. Even today, Spanish may be the language of the political system, the mass media, the legal system and the public administration, but Guaraní is the preferred language of the majority. Despite the historical bias towards Spanish in terms of the State (including attempts to eradicate Guaraní), 59% of Paraguayans still feel more comfortable speaking in Guaraní, (according to the 2002 census), a figure that rises to 83% in rural areas. Or put in another way, 88% of the population speak Guaraní whilst only 50% speak Spanish. In a complex and confusing relationship, Spanish is clearly the 'language of power', but Guaraní is the 'language of the people', spoken by the majority.

This characteristic is one that affects Paraguayans' ways of seeing and expressing the world around them and their place within it. Quite simply, it contributes to a sense of uniqueness and *paraguayidad*, as well as a strong sense of difference. Having two languages (bi-lingualism) creates the phenomenon of duality or dual personality, of different ways of expressing and interacting. Bilingualism (or more precisely in this case, diglossia) creates the phenomenon of duality or dual personality, of different ways of expressing and interacting. Moreover, there is a marked difference between bilingualism in say French and Spanish, on the one hand, and Spanish (modern) and Guaraní (pre-Columbian) on the other. Paraguayans are therefore tied to both pre-Columbian and modern roots, subject not just to a communication but also to a cultural split. Strikingly, however, according to the 2002 census, about 6% of the population speak only Spanish. That they are excluded from much of Paraguayan cultural expression is unfortunate; that they are generally the elites who dominate much of the world of business, politics, and government is a telling reflection of the structures of power still prevalent in Paraguay.

Land: The words poverty (*mboriahú*) and land (*yvy*) resonate in poetic and cultural terms far more in Guaraní than in Spanish. From colonial times, lack of international trade, the absence of lucrative natural (especially mineral) resources and economic mismanagement have meant that Paraguay has remained comparatively poor and underdeveloped. Such poverty has often been accepted and even romanticized in popular culture, from poetry to song. The reality, however, is that great pockets of wealth exist alongside widespread poverty: Paraguay, despite its own self-image, is not the poorest country in Latin America, but it does rank among the most unequal.

This inequality is best demonstrated in the issue of land. Paraguay until recently was predominantly rural, with the land (*la tierra colorada*) seen as a key feature of *paraguayidad.* When populist presidential candidate Lino Oviedo said in 1997, *jake jevy okape* ("*we will all once again sleep in the open air*") he touched upon a deep-rooted desire to be in close contact and harmony with nature, to be at one with the land, and on a more popular level, be able to be on one's own land, sipping *tereré*, swinging gently on a hammock in the shade of the mango tree. Acquisition of land has also traditionally been — and still is — a symbol of wealth and success, whether for politicians, the military, businessmen or contrabandistas. Indeed, although Paraguay has often, quite accurately, been described as a 'land without people and a people without land', in reference to the high levels of inequality, concentration of land and landlessness, land still very much forms part of the 'Paraguayan dream', the shared aspiration to have one's own piece of land.

Conclusion

It can be argued that the quest for any official national identity is a romanticized ideal, based more on the need to unite a population in a shared vision, than to seek an objective interpretation of history. This may well be the story of Paraguay. Highly-charged political nationalism has helped to shape her story even if it is on the decline in Paraguay and arguably was never a true reflection of national identity. Instead, to gain any understanding of *paraguayidad* we need to look at the country's geographical isolation, warfare, poverty and inequality, land, language and immigration: influences that have combined to shape the development of national culture and society and create a strong sense of shared identity. These influences have not only helped create deeply-rooted, shared cultural references which are uniquely Paraguayan, but also represent marked differences from her neighbours. Paraguayans, like most other countries, may be divided in many ways and there may well be no 'ser nacional'. However, this does not mean that there are not multiple identities and ways of being, which are tied together and enriched by shared experience and memory. These in turn have created a strong set of cultural bonds and references, and a popular sense of identity, or *ñandé rekó*, which are uniquely Paraguayan. ●

In the lands that make up Paraguay today, on either side of the Paraguay River, a variety of indigenous nations co-existed at times friendly, at times warring when European adventurers entered these lands in the early 1500s. Spanish and Portuguese explorers were trying to find and secure a route from the Atlantic to the vast wealth of silver in the Andes; they had little or no interest in the land that now forms Paraguay itself. They had heard from local tribes of the silver mountains of the Andes even before news of Pizarro's conquering advance into Peru reached Spain in 1534. It was only when these early explorers found that other groups of Spaniards had seized control of this vast mineral wealth that they felt obliged to settle in Paraguay, amidst what was by then a hostile Indian population.

The Indians of Paraguay

The local tribes were well-informed about the river routes to the Atlantic ocean, about the treasures of the high Andes, and about the difficult tracks through the desert wastes of the Chaco. Several Indian nations had been in continuous contact with each other across the Chaco in the pre-Colombian period (that is before the 'discovery' of the Americas by Christopher Columbus in 1492). These groups co-existed sometimes at war sometimes at peace in the century before the Europeans arrived, and even sometimes moving to fresh locations. The Terenos on the upper Paraguay (often called the Guaná or the Chané) came originally from the lands west of the Chaco. Another group, the Chiriguanos, had settled in the foothills of the Andes although they had come originally from the Paraguay River. In their lands to the west of Santa Cruz de la Sierra (in today's Bolivia), they lived in the valleys, according to the archaeological evidence, while the Peruvian Incas occupied the higher ground.

The first moments of contact on the Paraguay, in the 1520s and 1530s, followed a pattern already established by Cortes and his conquistadores in Mexico and Pizarro in Peru, they were just another small group of strangers who might be welcomed or rejected according to their actions. The Payaguas, the Guaycurús and the Guaraní were the first three groups to encounter the

MEETING ON THE RIVER:

THE FIRST CONTACT BETWEEN NATIVE INDIANS AND EUROPEANS

Richard Gott

Europeans, though many of these Indian nations came under different names and with attendant sub-tribes. The first two remained consistent in their hostility over subsequent centuries, while the Guaraní initially appeared both amiable and even submissive (a stance that they were soon to regret and were later to correct).

The water-based Payaguas (often called the Agaces) controlled and blocked access to the rivers (and gave their name to Paraguay); the nomadic Guaycurús (sometimes called the Mbaya), operating in the trackless wastes of the Chaco desert west of the Paraguay River, were able to close off the access routes to the silver-rich Andes;

the Guaraní (often called the Carios), on the east bank of the river, were already a settled agricultural people, occupying a wide area in what is today's Paraguay, northern Argentina, southern Brazil, and Uruguay.

Early cooperation

Initially, the Guaraní treated the Europeans well, sharing their food and their women in exchange for small gifts brought from across the Atlantic, chiefly knives and fish-hooks. They perceived the newcomers as potential allies against their own local enemies (the Payaguas and the Guaycurús). Although the Europeans' weapons, especially the gun, were unusual and surprising, they were also invariably rusty and inefficient and with damp powder did not initially have much of an advantage over bows and arrows fired by skilled archers. Their most alarming 'war machine' was the horse, brought to South America by the conquistadores. Yet soon the Guaycurús in particular, took advantage of this admirable animal, enabling them to move at unaccustomed speed across their Chaco homeland and to transform their fighting abilities.

The great weaknesses of the Europeans, immediately realized and taken advantage of by the Guaraní, lay in their unfamiliarity with the terrain, their inability to forage for food, their desire for women, their own rivalries and quarrels, and their lack of a respected *cacique* (leader) of their own. The Europeans were at the mercy of Indian guides, and the early death or departure of their most promising and authoritative leaders often led to political arguments that destroyed their capacity for decisive action. Yet many Indians were initially happy to cooperate with them. When the European adventurers sought Indian help in mounting large expeditions across the northern Chaco towards the Andes, many (from among the Guaraní, the Terenos and the Payaguas) were persuaded to join in. They knew about the distant treasure, they were familiar with the difficult routes, and they hoped to profit from the journey. They too had always been interested in the gold and silver of the Andes. With European help, they could hope to prevail over hostile Chaco nations, like the Guaycurús, who had always made the journey dangerous.

In spite of their eagerness, the Guaraní were never true allies. Their tactic was to be supportive on the way out and to rebel on the way home, sometimes killing the conquistadors and stealing their collected treasure. Subsequently, for most of the post-conquest period, many of them resolutely refused to give any assistance at all, and this became an important part of their resistance struggle. The paths across the Chaco were effectively closed for two centuries, until rediscovered by Jesuit missionaries in the middle of the 18th century.

Paraguay obscured

The story of the Spanish occupation of South America first became accessible to wider Western audiences through the 19th century writings of W.H. Prescott, the American historian. Prescott wrote in the 1840s about Hernán Cortés' conquest of Mexico in 1521 and about Francisco Pizarro's conquest of Peru in 1532. His histories left a lasting legacy on generations of schoolteachers and their students. Yet Paraguay, the third leg of the three-fold Spanish attack on the Americas in the 16th century, never received the same attention. Which is odd, because Paraguay attracted a similar list of heroic Spanish adventurers, a comparable collection of impressive Indian leaders, and several excellent observers who wrote down what they saw and experienced.

Paraguay's story is not only far less familiar than those of Mexico and Peru, but also very different. The Europeans in Paraguay established a more complex relationship with the Indians, based initially on interdependence and accommodation rather than slavery and rape. Crucially, the early history of Paraguay missed the vital ingredient of gold and silver, the treasuries of the Aztecs and the Incas that made the other histories so compelling and so bloody. Yet it was not for want of trying by a succession of ambitious conquistadors.

Spanish steps

The first Europeans to arrive on the Paraguay, Aleixo García in 1524 and Sebastian Cabot in 1527, believed that they had found the western back entrance to Peru, and they were well aware of the silver that would await them if they could get there. The adventurers that followed them — Juan de Ayolas and Domingo de Irala who arrived in 1536 and Alvar Núñez Cabeza de Vaca in 1542 — also made plans to cross the Chaco from the upper Paraguay, and head for the Andes. They too hoped to arrive at the silver mountains, an objective they had been given specific orders to achieve by the Spanish Emperor Charles V. For Spain to secure the silver of Peru via the Atlantic side of the continent, instead of through the Caribbean and the Panamanian isthmus, must initially have seemed a faster and safer route. Yet it was not to be.

During the first decade of the Spanish presence on the Paraguay, the westward expeditions were all a failure. Not until 1547 did Irala, by then the pre-eminent Spanish cacique (leader) in Paraguay, finally reach the higher slopes of the Andes. To his dismay, he had been forestalled by Spaniards advancing from the north, from Cuzco and Lima. The treasures of Peru were to be forever closed to the adventurers from Paraguay, a development with important implications for the Spaniards as well as for their future relations with the Indians with whom they shared this limited geographical space.

The Payaguas, Guaycurús and Guaranís

The most powerful opponents of the Spanish adventurers in the early years of conquest were the Payaguas. Their fleets of canoes controlled access to the Paraguay River, opposing and sometimes preventing Spanish ships from moving up from the River Plate to the Paraguay and the Paraná. The Spaniards described the Payaguas as "atrocious pirates", and most Europeans who first sought to enter Paraguay were obliged to travel by land from the Atlantic coast at Santa Catarina (an island across from the Brazilian city of Florianópolis).

The Payaguas held their own for 250 years, until the end of the 18th century. Martin Dobrizhoffer, a Jesuit missionary of that time, wrote of their weapons — bows and arrows, clubs, and long spears — but he considered their boats to be more formidable. *"Each family has its canoe, a narrow one indeed, but very long. They are managed with a single oar, pointed at the end like a sword, and fly at the slightest impulse in any direction."* [1]

---

[1] Martin Dobrizhoffer, *An Account of the Abipones, an equestrian people of Paraguay*, London, 1822, vol.2, p.422

The Payaguas had two kinds of canoe, one for fishing, their principal peacetime activity, the other for war. Their war canoes were large, with space for 40 fighting men. "*There is not perhaps a more dangerous nation on the face of the earth,*" wrote Pierre Francois Charlevoix, another 18th century Jesuit historian, though one without personal experience. "*They cover the most savage dispositions with the most engaging manners, and never make greater protestations of friendship than when they are treacherously meditating some mischief.*" [2] The early Spanish conquistadors would have recognised the description.

The second powerful opponents of the Spanish were the Chaco-based Guaycurús,[3] who made a profound impression on Cabeza de Vaca. "*These Indians are great warriors and valiant men,*" he reported. They spend much time in hunting and "*go daily to the chase for it is their only occupation. They are nimble and vigorous, swift of foot, and so long-winded that they tire out the deer, and catch them with their hands.*"[4]

The Guaycurús, according to this account, were much feared by other tribes, but uncommonly respectful to women: "*if any fall into their hands when they are making war, they set them at liberty and do them no wrong.*" Cabeza de Vaca noted the Guaycurús' healthy diet: "*they live on venison, butter, honey, fish and wild boar, eating nothing besides, neither they nor their wives and children.*"

The third major group encountered by the Spaniards, the Guaraní, lived on the east bank of the Paraguay River when the Spaniards first arrived. The Guaraní alone survived the European conquest with their language and much of their culture intact. They proved initially more sympathetic to the Spaniards than the Payaguas or the Guaycurús, but not for long.

Aleixo García and Sebastian Cabot

The first European to reach the Paraguay River was Aleixo García, a Portuguese adventurer. He travelled there by land in 1524 with five other Europeans from Santa Catarina. This had long been a familiar route to the local Indians, connecting the Guaraní on the Paraguay with those who lived on the Atlantic coast. García knew of the Andean silver and had learnt the Guaraní language while marooned for several years in Brazil. When he reached the upper Paraguay, he recruited a large contingent of 2,000 Guaraní to join him in a journey across the Chaco in search of treasure. His small army travelled with some difficulty, searching for food and fighting off the hostile Guaycurús.

García's expedition eventually arrived at the frontiers of the Inca empire, but could not progress to the well-defended silver mines in the Andes. They had to make do with acquiring considerable amounts of metal from

---

[2] Pierre François Charlevoix, *The History of Paraguay*, London, 1769, vol.1, p.51

[3] Other Chaco groups related to the Guaycurús that appear in the records of missionaries were the Caduveo, the Abipones, the Mocoví, the Pilaga, and the Tobá. Of these, only the Pilaga and the Tobá have survived into the 21st century, chiefly in the Argentine Chaco. "No seas un Guaycurú," is an admonition still made by some parents in northern Argentina to unruly children.

[4] "The Commentaries of Alvar Núñez Cabeza de Vaca", in Luís Domínguez (ed), *The Conquest of the River Plate*, Hakluyt Society, London, 1891

intermediaries, before returning across the Chaco by a different route and re-crossing the Paraguay River. García sent word (and some treasure) back to Santa Catarina, requesting assistance to mount a further expedition back to Peru, but it was not to be. The Payaguas on the river saw no reason to befriend this adventurer or the ill and hungry survivors of his troop, and they killed him.

García was followed in 1527 by Sebastian Cabot, a Venetian seaman, the first European to sail up the River Plate to Paraguay. He too had conflicts with the Payaguas, but he also encountered Indians with silver and heard stories of the treasures of Peru and of the Caracaraes, the "Charcas" people of the Andes. He was told of the existence of tracks through the Chaco. Cabot gave the great waterway he thought he had discovered the name of "the Silver River", but his further ambitions were frustrated by the arrival of a rival Spanish fleet led by Diego García. While the Europeans quarrelled, the Payaguas destroyed the base that Cabot had constructed at Sancti Spíritus (in northern Argentina). The two fleets were obliged to sail home to Spain with little to show for their efforts. The Indians had notched up a second victory.

A third and much larger European expedition to Paraguay was sent out in 1536, led by Pedro de Mendoza, an aristocrat from Granada. He sailed with a fleet of 14 ships, with 1,500 Spaniards on board, together with 150 Germans, a handful of Portuguese, and 72 horses. This was a major Spanish investment, inspired by the news of the silver discoveries in Peru and by fears that Spain's Portuguese rivals had plans to send ships to the River Plate. Mendoza's fleet established a base at Buenos Aires, at the entrance to the river, but they found themselves surrounded by hostile Indians who threatened to overwhelm them. Mendoza himself, the expedition's leader and financier, fell ill and was obliged to start for home. He died on the way back.

Juan de Ayolas and Domingo de Irala

With the illness and departure of the expedition's commander, two new leaders emerged: Juan de Ayolas from Burgos' and Domingo de Irala from the Basque Country. Also in the fleet was a competent German chronicler, Ulrich Schmidl, from Bavaria. Leaving a garrison behind at Buenos Aires, the Spanish ships set off up the Paraná and the Paraguay. Ayolas and Irala were sent on to the upper Paraguay with three small ships and 175 soldiers, to search for the route to the west, while a third Spanish officer, Juan de Sálazar, was left to build a military base at Asunción. This was on the east bank of the Paraguay in a densely populated zone, with perhaps 200,000 Guaraní settled in the neighbourhood in small communities.

The Guaraní cacique who controlled the land by the river at Asunción was called Caracará. To the south lived another cacique, Cupiratí, who was described as *"el principal sobre todos los principales"* (loosely 'chief of all the chiefs'). To the north were Timbuaí and Mayreru. Further north still, at the port of Tapúa, was Moquiracé, while at the entrance of the river Jejuí were two other caciques, Guacaní and Aracaré.[5] With all these caciques the Spaniards made successful alliances in the first few years, but they were tenuous at best.

---

[5] Florencia Roulet, *La Resistencia de los Guaraní del Paraguay a la Conquista Española*, Editorial Universitaria, Posadas, Misiones, 1993, pp.88-9

The Spaniards had to behave with some circumspection. They had fought their way up the lower part of the river against the Payaguas and their first reaction was to slaughter hostile natives. Yet they also needed to be on friendly terms with at least some of the local inhabitants, and the Guaraní were the most immediately friendly. The conquistadors depended upon them for food and provisions. Looking ahead, they recognised that they would need Guaraní camp followers if they were to embark again on the silver trail towards Peru. The Guaraní, for their part, were initially intrigued by these bearded newcomers, content to tolerate their presence, and happy to barter food for fish-hooks. They also hoped that the European force might prove a useful ally against their own immediate enemies.

The expedition on the upper Paraguay led by Ayolas and Irala was initially well received by the cacique of the Payaguas. He was perhaps impressed by the size of the Spanish force. "*The cacique met us peaceably*", Schmidl reported, "*and took us into their houses and gave us fish*". Food was the primary need of the conquistadors, and the Payaguas, like the Guaraní downriver, were initially prepared to provide it, in exchange for knives and fish-hooks. The Payaguas also presented Ayolas with a Tereno who claimed to have been the slave of Aleixo García.

Ayolas now embarked on a journey across the Chaco with the Tereno as his guide. He left Irala behind to guard his position on the river. The expedition set off in February 1537 with 135 of his own soldiers and 300 Payaguas. Some Terenos came too, to act as baggage handlers — and to help bring back the anticipated treasure. The Payagua cacique gave his blessing to the trip, presenting Ayolas with his daughter so that she might travel with him. Irala was told to await Ayolas' return, as was Schmidl, so no eye-witness account survives of Ayolas' actual journey.

Like García ten years earlier, Ayolas crossed the Rio Grande and reached the foothills of the Andes. He collected some treasure but came under attack from a superior force of "Charcas" Indians. Retreating across the Chaco to the Paraguay, after a two year expedition, he arrived back in the course of 1539. Eighty of his soldiers had survived, but all were ill and lacked munitions and powder, as well as food. Their accompanying Terenos, however, had brought "*twenty cargoes of metal*".

In the meantime, Domingo de Irala had travelled up and down the river to Asunción several times, waiting for Ayolas' return. Irala sailed up the river again in November 1539 with a more powerful force of 9 ships and 280 men. He came this time with Aracaré, the Guaraní cacique who had participated in the foundation of Asunción and who claimed to have knowledge of the trans-Chaco route. With Aracaré's help, Irala hoped to overawe the Payaguas and to make contact with Ayolas, now missing for two years. He came across six Payaguas in a canoe, one of whom claimed to have been with Ayolas. He was given the bleak news that a dozen Spaniards had returned with Ayolas bringing much metal, but all had been killed. Further investigation suggested that Ayolas' treasure had been too tempting; he had been set upon by a joint force of Payaguas and Guaycurús. According to Schmidt's account these Payaguas "*were compelled to confess that they had killed the Christians and their chief*". Two prisoners were then burnt alive, tied to a tree "*around which a great fire was made in order to burn them.*".

With the death of Ayolas, Irala was now the principal Spanish leader on the river. He returned to Asunción with his men faint from hunger. More than fifty had died. In Asunción the situation had become ever more bleak. A great plague of locusts had afflicted the town. Some of his followers had begun to question his leadership. And the Guaraní had grown unfriendly.

Cabeza de Vaca takes control

In March 1542, a new governor arrived in Asunción from Spain, a senior figure appointed to replace Pedro de Mendoza and one destined to clash with Irala. The Spanish authorities sent out the famous Alvar Núñez Cabeza de Vaca, a conquistador of the generation of Cortés and Pizarro who had already made a name for himself in the 1520s by travelling through Florida to Mexico. Cabeza de Vaca arrived with another large Spanish contingent, with 400 men and 30 horses. Like García before him, he avoided the river route controlled by the Payaguas and travelled across from Santa Catarina by land.

In Asunción, he found a leaderless and disaffected group of 350 Spaniards. They had been living there for five years, long out of contact with Spain. They had begun to lose hope that they would ever receive assistance, for they had run out of trinkets and were no longer able to barter for food. Relations with the Guaraní were at a low ebb. Their hopes of travelling to the silver mountains seemed forever postponed.

Immediately on arrival, Cabeza de Vaca was caught up in a renewal of the age-old conflict between Guaraní and Guaycurús. He had brought supplies of knives and fish-hooks with him, and was able again to barter food for the Spanish population, but clearly the only way to recover the support and confidence of the Guaraní was to join with them in making war on the Guaycurús. Since the Guaraní now considered themselves to be vassals of the Spanish monarch, they said, they thought it was right to claim "protection and restitution of their property."

Almost wholly unprepared, Cabeza de Vaca was now obliged to engage in the first large-scale Spanish battle fought in this part of the world. When the army of Spaniards and Guaraní marched out of Asunción and crossed the river to the Chaco side, it was an impressive sight. In front were the Guaraní "*numbering some 10,000 men, all painted and bedizened with necklaces of beads and plumes, and plates of copper which glistened marvellously well in the sun.*"[6] The Spaniards followed, with Cabeza de Vaca himself and twelve men on horseback, followed by 200 arquebusiers (firearms) and crossbowmen. "*After these came the women, bearing the munitions and provisions of the Spaniards. The Indians carried their own supplies.*"

The Guaraní were uncertain whether this impressive band would be adequate to defeat the warlike Guaycurús, and at nightfall they began to slip away. Cabeza de Vaca called them back. "*You know that the war we are about to engage in is in your interest and on your behalf only, for the Guaycurús have never seen the Spaniards or had any trouble or grievance with them. We are proceeding against them to protect and defend you.*"

When they reached the settlement of the Guaycurús the next day, "*the Guaraní were almost paralysed with fear; nothing would induce them to begin the attack.*" In the subsequent battle, 1,000 Guaraní were killed and 400

---

[6] "The Commentaries of Alvar Núñez Cabeza de Vaca"

Guaycurús were taken prisoner. The Spaniards had a trump card, for when the Guaycurús suddenly became aware of the horses, "*a great fear fell upon them, and they fled to the mountains as fast as they could.*"

The Guaraní were so pleased with this victory that when Cabeza de Vaca sent Irala upriver again a few months later, in October 1542, he was accompanied once more by the reliable Guaraní cacique Aracaré. On this occasion, Irala headed further north, eventually halting at Lake Gaiba, north of Corumbá in what is now the Pantanal. He came on a scouting expedition with three luggers (small sailing vessels) and 90 Europeans. Yet this expedition was as fruitless as the earlier ones, more so because of the deviousness of Aracaré. Moving into the Chaco, he roused the Guaycurús to kill the Spaniards and to block their movements. Hearing of this, Cabeza de Vaca gave orders that Aracaré should be executed, a mission rapidly accomplished by Irala, before returning to Asunción in February 1543.

Yet it seemed that Irala had usefully reconnoitred a fresh route into the Chaco, and later in the year, in September 1543, Cabeza de Vaca himself set off upriver from Asunción, travelling with the largest group assembled so far. He sailed with 10 luggers, with 400 Spaniards and 10 horses on board, accompanied by 1,200 Guaraní in 120 canoes. He came to anchor at Lake Gaiba, and from there, with a Guaraní guide, he set off on a trackless journey to the west.

Within a week, the difficulties of earlier expeditions were repeated. The guide confessed that he was lost, it was many years since he had made the journey. The Spaniards fell ill and grew rebellious. A majority wished to give up. Surrounded by faint-hearts and malcontents, Cabeza de Vaca was forced to return, first to Lake Gaiba and then to Asunción. Within days of his arrival, in March 1544, he was arrested by Irala's supporters, imprisoned, and sent back to Spain

Irala' coup

It was the first coup d'etat in Paraguay, master-minded by Irala, and now the unchallenged commander. He prepared yet again to find the way across the Chaco to the elusive silver mines of Peru, but it was another three years, in 1547, before he was ready to make a new expedition, rather smaller and more compact than before. He sailed north from Asunción with 7 ships carrying 250 Spaniards and 27 horses, with 200 Indians in 200 canoes. This time he took no chances with the Payaguas, constructing a fort on the upper Paraguay to guard against them. Adequate provisions were stored there for a lengthy siege.

Irala's expeditionary force eventually arrived at the outskirts of La Plata (today the town of Sucre in Bolivia). To his great surprise, his men encountered some Indians speaking Spanish. He was soon to discover that the whole of this region of Upper Peru — today's Bolivia — was already controlled by other Spanish conquistadores. In fact La Plata had been established nearly ten years earlier by Pedro Anzures, one of Francisco Pizarro's lieutenants. The Inca city of Cuzco had been captured by Pizarro in 1533 and the treasure of Atahualpa had already been seized and taken to Spain. The silver mountain of Potosí had been discovered by Gonzalo Pizarro in 1542, although not exploited until 1545.

Anxious to clarify the situation, Irala sent Nuflo de Chávez, one of his own trusted officers, to Lima, to negotiate with Pedro de la Gasca, the Spanish Viceroy. The Viceroy's message was clear. Irala and his men were ordered to return to the Paraguay River. He was told in no uncertain terms to keep out. The silver mines were to be controlled from Lima, not from Asunción. The Paraguayan dream of instant riches was over.

Settling down with the Guaraní

The small group of Europeans huddled together in a small fort at Asunción would continue to gaze across to the other side of the river, and to dream of further expeditions to the west, but their principal task was now to establish themselves as settlers in lands occupied by others. This was not what they had originally come to do, and they were largely unprepared for the difficulties ahead. While the Guaraní on the east bank of the river had initially been friendly, by mid-century they had joined other powerful local nations in opposing the Spanish settlement. They had good reason. The new aim of the Spaniards was to enslave the Indians, to take their land and to seize their women, and to replace the Guaraní as the preponderant political force in the region.

Yet an unforeseen development began to alter the relationship between the Spaniards and the Indians in the years ahead. Guaraní women in the area of Asunción were accustomed in their own society to perform a variety of tasks. They cultivated the land, they harvested the crops and they prepared the food. This was the local practice. The men, meanwhile, went out to hunt and to fish.

A woman's work was by no means confined to the field and the kitchen, for it was the custom for women to be handed over to others. Caciques were often free with the women of their own nation, giving them away as prizes or bribes, or simply as a gesture of friendship. The female Guaraní were not of course party to these arrangements. No one asked them if they wished to be the companions of the incoming Europeans. Less warlike than the Guaycurús or the Payaguas, the Guaraní men succumbed to Spanish power in the early years almost without a fight. Surrendering their women caused them little disquiet; it was to be a much repeated pattern in Spanish settlement.

Yet to present every male Spaniard with a Guaraní woman, to grow and prepare his food, did of course have other consequences. Few Spanish women came in the early fleets of the invaders, and Asunción was soon a town filled with *mestizo* children, the progeny of the Spaniards and their Guaraní companions. When the Spaniards first arrived in 1537, they numbered about 250 and soon they had more than 700 Guaraní women at their disposal: about three women to each man, a low ratio by all accounts. A Spanish chaplain wrote to the king in 1545 to explain the situation: "*Here some have up to seventy women; if you are poor, you may have five or six; most have fifteen or twenty; or even forty or fifty.*"[7] Asunción was referred to in early reports as "the paradise of Mahomet", and there were references to the fact that even "the Koran of Mahomet" would not have given permission for what was going on. The Spaniards of course had expelled the Moslems from Spain a mere half a century earlier; memories of a many-wived Moslem male lifestyle was still a recent folk memory. In such a way was the vision of a Paraguayan arcadia built up in the earliest years.

---

[7] Enrique de Gandia, *Indios y Conquistadores en el Paraguay*, Buenos Aires, 1932

The Mestizo mix and the Indian nations' dramatic decline

By 1545, within seven years of its foundation and after the arrival of reinforcements with Cabeza de Vaca in 1542, the number of Spaniards living in Asunción had risen to 600, and among them were 1500 *mestizo* children.[8] Ten years later, in 1556, there were more than 4000 *mestizo* boys and girls,[9] and by 1575, nearly forty years after the first European settlement, some 10,000 *mestizo* teenagers were on the prowl in Asunción. By all accounts they were unruly and unmanageable, uncertain where their loyalties lay.[10]

From the 1550 onwards, the Guaraní and the other Indian nations of Paraguay maintained an almost permanent state of rebellion, while the Spaniards grew increasingly violent in their determination to crush them. Their efforts were eventually successful. Over the years, the Indians began to disappear from the story. They fled into the more distant forests, they were captured and enslaved by the Portuguese from Brazil, ever on the warpath on the eastern border, they died of disease, and their women increasingly practiced abortion and infanticide. Anthropologist Pierre Clastres has estimated that there were 1,500,000 Indians in the area between the Atlantic and the Paraguay river when the Spaniards first arrived in the 1530s. By 1730, 200 years later, there were barely 150,000: a ten-fold decline.[11] Only among the heirs to the *mestizos* was something preserved of the culture and the language of the original inhabitants. ●

[8] Florencia Roulet, La Resistencia de los Guaraní del Paraguay, p.23

[9] Florencia Roulet, La Resistencia de los Guaraní del Paraguay, p.228

[10] Branislava Susnik, El Indio Colonial del Paraguay, vol.1, El Guaraní Colonial, Museo Étnico Andrés Barbero, Asunción, 1965

[11] Pierre Clastres, Society against the State: essays in political anthropology, Zone Books, New York, 1989, quoted in Richard Gott, Land Without Evil: Utopian Journeys across the South American Watershed, Verso, London, 1993

PARAGUAY'S HYDROELECTRIC POWER *Diana McClure*

Paraguay is in the centre of South America, and its international borders are mostly formed by rivers. It has two major bi-national hydroelectric power stations: both are on the River Parana ('Mighty River' in Guaraní): Itaipú lies on Paraguay's eastern border with Brazil, and Yacyreta is on its south-eastern border with Argentina.

Itaipú ('Singing Stone' in Guaraní) is the largest hydroelectric station in the world (in terms of power output). In 1994 the American Society of Civil Engineers, in celebration of monumental engineering and construction feats of the 20th century, elected it as one of the seven wonders of the modern world. Completed in 1991, it took 16 years to build and it used 15 times more concrete than the Channel Tunnel. It is run by Brazil and Paraguay, and it generates 90% of the energy used by Paraguay and 19% of that used by Brazil. The installed generation capacity of the plant is 14 GW (gigawatts), with 20 generating units providing 700 MW (megawatts) each. Itaipú generated 94.7 GWh (Gigawatt/hours — a world record) in 2008 and 91.6 GWh in 2009. The maximum flow of Itaipú's 14 segmented spillways is 62.2 thousand cubic metres per second, into three ski-slope-shaped canals. It is equivalent to 40 times the average flow of the nearby natural world-famous Iguazu Falls.

By the terms of a treaty signed in 1973, Paraguay is obliged to sell the surplus electricity it does not require to Brazil, at a fixed price, until 2023. There has always been widespread discontent in Paraguay over the terms of this treaty, and in 2009 the President of Brazil agreed to a fairer payment to Paraguay, and also to allow Paraguay to sell excess power directly to Brazilian companies instead of solely through the Brazilian electricity monopoly. However, by October 2010 the Brazilian Congress had not ratified the agreement.

The Itaipú dam is 7,235 metres long and 196 metres high: 1,350 square kilometres were flooded by the reservoir, and 10,000 families living beside the Parana River were displaced. The reservoir completely submerged extensive tracts of jungle on the Paraguayan side, farmland on the Brazilian side, and the Guairá Falls, a series of

Yacyreta Dam.

massive waterfalls with an estimated volume of 1,750,000 cubic feet per second. They were the world's largest waterfall by volume, and one of the natural wonders of the world. The rock face which formed the falls was dynamited, in order to make for safer navigation. This has eliminated the possibility of restoring the falls in the future. The Itaipú dam is 15 km north of the Puente de la Amistad (Friendship Bridge), which crosses the River Parana between Ciudad del Este in Paraguay and Foz de Iguaçu in Brazil.

Yacyreta hydroelectric power station (from the Guaraní *jasy reta* 'country of the moon' and like Itaipú, named after an island in the Parana) is built over the waterfalls of Yacyreta-Apipe in the Parana River, on the border between Argentina and Paraguay. The dam is 808 metres long and has a maximum power output of 4,050 MW, with an annual maximum power output of 19,080 GWh, and a maximum water flow rate of 55,000 cubic metres per second. Because the reservoir is seven metres below its planned water level, the dam currently operates at only 60% capacity. At present, the reservoir covers 1,600 square kilometres and has displaced 40,000 people. When the dam is completed and the water level were to rise by seven metres, another 500 square kilometres of land would be flooded, and 80,000 people would be displaced.

The project generated controversy during its planning and construction because of the delays, the cost, and the effect it had on local ecology, particularly the flooding of a unique environment causing the extinction of some species. It has also caused flooding of many houses in low-lying parts of Encarnación, in Paraguay, and of Posadas, in Argentina. It has cost about 11 billion dollars to build Yacyreta — more than five times the original budget of two billion dollars.

With the completion of these two hydroelelctric schemes, Paraguay has become not only self-sufficient in the production of clean electricity but also one of the few countries capable of exporting hydroelectric energy in the world.

Yacyreta and Itaipú plants.

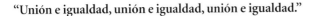

"Unión e igualdad, unión e igualdad, unión e igualdad."

Not even a foreigner can fail to hear and understand these repeated words of the national anthem, sung with fervour and solemnity at so many events, and taught to schoolchildren right from kindergarten. The *himno nacional* calls up from deep in the Paraguayan soul the people's pride in their independence: we were oppressed by a foreign power, says the verse, beginning in slow and stately fashion, until we rose up and said "enough!" And so, the chorus continues, in now rapidly triumphant fashion "Neither tyrants nor slaves can continue, Where unity and equality reign."

Yet that sense of national unity was not always there. In the beginnings of Paraquaria — the Latin name of the Jesuit province founded in 1605-7, which preceded the nation of Paraguay, and subsequently turned into the name of the country — the division between oppressed and oppressors ran along the demarcation line of the Jesuit-Guaraní 'Reductions' (missionary towns or reserves), which was a quite different border from that of today's nation. Though loosely referred to in a collective way as the Paraguayan Reductions, the Treinta Pueblos of Paraquaria (in their developed phase after the migrations from Guairá and Itatín) covered the south of present-day Paraguay and extended over what are now the provinces of Corrientes and Misiones, Argentina, and into the state of Missōes in present-day Brazil.

THE JESUITS' INFLUENCE IN NATIONAL IDENTITY

Margaret Hebblethwaite

The Reductions formed a buffer-state, between the Portuguese to the east and the Spanish to the west, who after the first generation were no longer just the Portuguese and the Spanish, but the American-born *criollos* and the mixed-race *mamelucos* and *mestizos*. Sadly these were just as much oppressors as the *conquistadores* had been. The *mamelucos* (mixed-race second-generation Portuguese) came to hunt the Guaraní to sell as slaves and to extend Portuguese territory. Those under Spanish rule were not supposed to have slaves but effectively practised slavery under another name, the enforced hard-labour of the *encomienda* system that operated in the Asunción region.

At that date, independence would not have helped the original inhabitants, for it was the Spanish crown that gave authority to the Jesuits to ban those who were not indigenous from the region of the *Treinta Pueblos*, and so protect the people from the exploitation and oppression of those coming both from São Paulo and from Asunción. If visitors needed to come in for serious reasons such as commerce, their stay would be restricted to three days. The Reductions, kept clear in this way from the vices of alcohol, prostitution and exploitative labour practices, were able to flourish in an amazing way.

On the facade of the Ruins of Jesús today, you can see two niches that once housed statues of Saints Peter and Paul. St Peter's niche is topped with a papal tiara and two crossed keys, and St Paul's with the tiara and two crossed swords. Far from meaning that the armed invasion of the Americas was blessed by the Church, this meant the opposite — that the Church protects the right of this place to defend itself by arms if necessary. The same message is enshrined in the name that the Jesuit saint and martyr Roque González de Santa Cruz gave to a painting of the Virgin Mary that he used to carry with him, *La Virgen Conquistadora*: it is not that the Guaraní are conquered by the Europeans with the blessing of the Virgin, but on the contrary, that the Virgin, who is on their side, is always victorious.

The Reductions flourish

The high period of freedom for the Reductions began after the decisive victory of the Guaraní against the slave hunters in the 1641 Battle of Mbororé. The Guaraní victory was thanks to the new permission given by the Spanish crown for them to carry firearms, a permission not normally given to native peoples for fear that they would rise up against their European masters. This led to a more settled atmosphere for the foundation from the 1690s onwards of new Reductions in Chiquitos and Moxos (Bolivia) — for other indigenous peoples, but closely modelled on the Guaraní prototypes.

With the harassment of slave-hunting removed, a civilisation began to grow up in the Misiones territory that was in advance of what was being achieved either in São Paulo or in Asunción. The Spanish and creole population, looking on jealously from the distance of Asunción, were resentful of the fact that the people they regarded as savages could have reached this level of development by sheer hard work. The Jesuit-Guaraní culture was superior to theirs — architecturally, artistically, musically, economically and agriculturally, not to mention spiritually.

When you consider that there were only two Jesuits in each Reduction, among a population of three or four thousand, it is evident that the Jesuits could do little more than teach skills for others to carry on, and that the civilisation flourished by Guaraní hard work and talent, but under Jesuit tutelage and protection. Nonetheless, among the Jesuits were men of extraordinary abilities, who would have had outstanding careers in Europe if they had not decided to entrust their lives wholly to God: composers and writers, agriculturalists and astronomers, botanists and musicians, painters and architects. If anything in the history of Paraguay could be seen as an expression of *unión e igualdad*, it was the decision of these men to sacrifice careers in the developed world in favour of uniting themselves with a remote and persecuted people, regarded as semi-human by their oppressors, but by the Jesuits as human beings of equal rights and dignity.

The contemporary accounts wax lyrical about the splendour of the churches in the Reductions, and we still have the Ruins of Trinidad and Jesús and some surviving buildings in San Cosme y Damián. The carved wooden statues of saints, Christ and the Virgin, found in the museums of San Ignacio, Santa María de Fe, Santa Rosa and Santiago, include impressive works of art, with extraordinarily powerful facial expressions. The large Plazas, used for magnificent flower-adorned processions, sporting events and performances of operatic works, still form focal points in the Paraguayan Reductions that can be visited today.

As for the music, the Guaraní choirs which rendered the baroque polyphony of Domenico Zipoli and anonymous Guaraní composers, were said by contemporary reports to "sing with such harmony, fullness and devotion that it is enough to make the hardest heart tender... and many of their voices would shine in the best cathedrals of Europe" (18th-century Jesuit José Cardiel). A number of recordings have been made of this religious music of the Reductions, by Paraguayan conductor Luis Szarán and others, but there is a special verve and freshness when this music is sung by the indigenous people, as by the talented group from San Ignacio de Moxos, Bolivia (another Jesuit Reduction, but beyond the Guaraní region).

Life within the Reductions

Unión e igualdad were key concepts for life in the Reductions: everyone had to work, and no one was able to sit back and profit from the labour of others. Cash currency within the *pueblos* did not exist, but every family had its allotted allowance of land, its ration of meat, and shared use of oxen according to their needs. The Reductions had a highly organised community structure, and every worker had to devote a couple of days a week to the *Tupã Mba'e* — "God's thing" — that is, work for the community to support the vulnerable members of society, and to provide produce that could be sold outside the Reduction and cover the costs of imports. *Yerba mate* — the "green gold" of Paraguay — was a major export, but its large-scale production required great knowledge and skill, and was a particular Jesuit-Guaraní achievement.

Looking back on that time, Carlos Bedoya, the historian from San Ignacio Guasú (itself the oldest Reduction, founded in 1609), gave an inspiring lecture in 2005 in the *Instituto* of Santa María de Fe, in which he described the *Treinta Pueblos* as a nation in itself, because it had five characteristics of national identity: its own language, its own political system, its own economic system, its own religion and its own identity-forming vision *(see also page 15)*.

The language in the areas invaded by the *conquistadores* was Spanish, but the people in the *Treinta Pueblos* spoke Guaraní and Latin (the language of church services, taught in the *colegios*, and a common language between Jesuits coming from all over Europe). The religion in the Reductions was Catholic, but it was so differently conceived and expressed from the Catholicism of the *conquistadores*, that the two groups hardly seemed to belong to the same Church.

The Guaraní had their own special vision — the *yvý marane'ÿ* or "land without evil" or *tierra sin mal*. This paradise, towards which the semi-nomadic people believed they were always moving, easily merged with the Jewish "Promised land" and the Christian "Kingdom of God". What they were achieving in the Reductions was already being acclaimed in Europe as "the perfect image of the primitive church" (by the Italian scholar L.A. Muratori), and (by the French philosopher Voltaire) as "perhaps the highest degree of civilisation to which it is possible to conduct a young people". By contrast, the vision that motivated the *conquistadores* was to discover a continent where they could make their fortune, with the gold of Peru and the silver believed to lie in the Rio de la Plata (River of Silver).

When the Jesuits were expelled from South America in 1768, the civilisation of the Reductions was destroyed almost overnight. The fortune-seekers from the Asunción region came in to occupy the best territory and to filch the best artworks. The Jesuit systems and structures were undermined, buildings fell into disrepair, field were uncultivated, and within eight years great hunger was reported. In 30 years the population had plummeted to half as the Guaraní abandoned the missions — not just fleeing back into the jungle but trying their luck in other populated areas. Those who looked on from afar saw it as the loss of a Utopia. *A Vanished Arcadia* was the title of R.B. Cunninghame Graham's book in 1901, inspired by interviews with Guaraní survivors. It made an impact in the English-speaking world, and formed the basis for Philip Caraman's subsequent work *The Lost Paradise* (1975, Sidgwick and Jackson).

The five marks of nationhood, have been absorbed into what became the wider nation, which has made a new sense of identity out of the synthesis. The political and economic systems have been lost, but the search for the "land without evil" is still hovering there dimly in the background, and the faith of the Guaraní can be seen in the remnants of religious statues and ruined churches, while the Catholic influence has sunk into the heartbeat of the new nation.

Legacy of the Guaraní language

But the most important living witness to the ongoing influence of the Reductions in the life of the nation is the Guaraní language. The bi-lingual character of Paraguay is of critical importance to national identity *(see also page 15)*, and its survival owes a lot to the fact that it was preserved pure and untampered by intermarriage in the *Treinta Pueblos* for the century-and-a-half duration of the Jesuit-Guaraní Reductions (1609 -1768). Not only that, but the Jesuits enabled it to be transformed from a purely oral language into a written language. Antonio Ruiz de Montoya wrote the first grammar and dictionary, the *Arte de la Lengua Guaraní* and the *Vocabulario de la Lengua Guaraní*, and his work has been carried on by other Jesuits, who right up to the present day play a leading role in Guaraní studies. The first Bible in Guaraní was translated by Jesuit Diego Ortiz (as recently as 1996); the standard grammar and dictionaries are works by another Jesuit Antonio Guasch (first published in the 1960s); Jesuit Bartomeu Melia continues to be one of the most prolific writers about the Guaraní language; and Jesuit Alberto Luna is one of the new generation of Guaraní promoters with his book of poems *Pypore* ("Footprint") published in 2008.

Resonances of the Jesuit-Guaraní Reductions

Paraguay has had a long and tragic history of tyrants and slaves, and the achievement of independence in 1811 — only 43 years after the Jesuit Expulsion — by no means put an end to tyrannies. In the midst of the longest dictatorship, that of Alfredo Stroessner (1954-89) a new Christian movement sprang up in Misiones, once again under the influence and encouragement of the Jesuits. The short-lived *Ligas Agrarias Cristianas* had extraordinary resonances with the Reductions that flourished some two centuries earlier in the same territory: they were founded in Misiones (in Santa Rosa, to be precise, in 1960); they were for the people at the base of society — in this case, for poor *campesinos* who had Guaraní from the Reductions as their ancestors; and they promoted sharing and solidarity (*mínga* and *jopói*) — in working the fields together, in organising cooperatives, and in forming independent schools teaching *campesino* values (the *Escuelitas Campesinas*).

The *Ligas* were based around biblical reflection groups and in particular the teaching of *hermandad* (brotherhood and sisterhood), which is at the heart of the Bible, and is one of the scriptural terms for unity and equality. The title of the book of liberation theology written by the Jesuit José Luis Caravias, out of this experience of the *Ligas* in Misiones, is *Vivir como Hermanos: reflexiones bíblicas sobre la hermandad* (first published in 1971 in Spain, when it was dangerous to publish in Paraguay; republished in Asunción by CEPAG in 2003). The sense of unity and equality given by *hermandad* undermined the traditional passivity of the *campesinos* that enabled a dictator to control the people, and the *Ligas Agrarias Cristianas* were always persecuted and harrassed by Stroessner's police. In Holy Week 1976 — known as the *Pascua Dolorosa* — the *Ligas* were violently wiped out and their leaders spent many years in prison suffering constant tortures.

There is a growing will to value and promote the legacy of the Jesuit-Guaraní Reductions, through, for example, the *Ruta Jesuítica* which is a programme promoted by the government tourist office Senatur. This is admirable and necessary, but there is as yet little interest in recovering the memory of the second Christian community base movement in Misiones, the *Ligas Agrarias*, about which knowledge is hazy and interest almost non-existent, despite the efforts of the recent *Comisión de Verdad y Justicia*, which delivered its report in 2008.

Even though there are still many surviving brothers and sisters who suffered the repression, the fear instilled by Stroessner's police achieved its effect of eliminating all discussion of these events. But unless there is a movement to recover and revalue the memory of the *Ligas*, the message of the Reductions and the injustice of the Expulsion will remain at the superficial level of a museum interest, and not as the assimilation of biblical values that are transformative, because they are constantly re-applied.

"Nunca más" ("Never again") is the refrain of those in all the Southern Cone countries who are involved in recovering the memory of the human-rights abuses under the various late 20th-century dictatorships. "Never again" is also the unspoken feeling of those who watch the shocking end of Roland Joffe's powerful film, *The Mission*, as they see the violent and mindless destruction of the Reductions for heartless political motives. In the bi-centenary of Paraguay as an independent nation, the message needs to sink in that Independence has no meaning and no effect if one system of tyrants and slaves is followed by another. ●

THE MOISÉS BERTONI FOUNDATION *Diane Espinoza and Yan Speranza*

". . . The Goddess Natura, beautiful and jealous, hides her lovely finery from those who do not faithfully and thoroughly admire her in the very theatre of her triumphs." Moisés Bertoni, 1914

The Foundation that has become an innovative model to promote environmental, social, and economic development in a conservation area of Paraguay, is named in honor of a Swiss scientist, naturalist, and scholar who lived in Paraguay from 1887 until his death in 1929.

Moisés Santiago Bertoni was one of a band of scientists that came to South America in the 19th century fascinated by the exotic novelty of the continent and the possibilities it offered for new discoveries and scientific advancement. Born in 1857, he left his native Switzerland in 1884 to pursue his ideal of a life in the New World with his entire family, including his mother Giuseppina Torreani, his wife Eugenia, who was a biochemist, and their children Reto, Winkelried, Vera, Sofía and Inés, the first five of 13 children.

Bertoni's mission was to establish a colony that would bring together agricultural production and scientific research. Some 40 farmers accompanied him in the venture. He first settled in Argentina but moved to Paraguay where he founded the *Colonia Guillermo Tell*, now called *Puerto Bertoni*. There he found the perfect environment to conduct his research and experiments.

Uncovering Paraguay's natural history secrets

Bertoni discovered and classified many new species of plants and left an impressive collection of more than 7000 plant species and about 6500 insect species. His research in botany, meteorology, and anthropology has been a great contribution to the scientific knowledge of the natural life in Paraguay. His work gave him both national and international recognition. One of the plants he studied in depth was *ka'a he'e (Stevia rebaudiana bertoni)*, which is an indigenous herb in Paraguay, and is important today as a non-caloric sweetener, reputed to be 300 times sweeter than sugar. He also scientifically classified Yerba Mate *(Ilex Paraguariensis)*.

In 1896, the President of Paraguay, Juan Bautista Egusquiza, invited him to establish the National School of Agriculture, which he directed for nine years. In 1903 he organised the National Society of Agriculture and in 1910 participated in the International Agricultural Exhibition in Buenos Aires where he was awarded several medals.

Bertoni is undoubtedly one of the most extraordinary immigrants ever to have settled in Paraguay where he was called *el Sabio Bertoni*. He died on 19th September, 1929, at the age of 72 in the city of Foz do Iguazu (Brazil).

The Foundation in action

The Moisés Bertoni Foundation manages the Mbaracayú Natural Forest Reserve, which is protected in perpetuity. The Mbaracayú Reserve consists of 64,400 hectares located in the northeast of Paraguay: it is the most important and largest continuous block of forest that remains unchanged within the unique and highly threatened ecosystem of the Atlantic Forest.

The strategy of the Foundation has gone much further than just the conservation of the protected area. An innovative model was created to promote the environmental, social, and economic development of the area, in an effort to overcome the inherent clash of nature conservation with people's livelihood. The Foundation wants to integrate conservation and sustainable development, and works actively with the local populations to acheive this aim.

The foundation has developed the following working model:

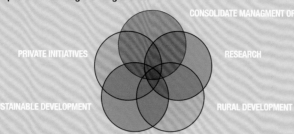

CONSOLIDATE MANAGMENT OF THE PROTECTED AREA

PRIVATE INITIATIVES

RESEARCH

EDUCATION FOR SUSTAINABLE DEVELOPMENT

RURAL DEVELOPMENT

These elements are inter-related and aim to transform the Mbaracayú Biosphere Reserve (340,000 hectares declared by UNESCO in 2000, the first biosphere reserve in Paraguay), into a region where sustainable development is becoming an achievable reality.

Consolidate management of the protected area. The Mbaracayú Reserve has remained protected and intact over the past 20 years and the Moisés Bertoni Foundation has extended its work to the buffer zone through active work with the local population, who have formed a Management Committee of the Biosphere Reserve. This focuses on the effective sustainable development of their territory.

Scientific research. Many projects have been developed in partnership with national and international research centres and universities. Such joint research allows a way to better understand the great wealth of biodiversity that is found in the region and its interaction with the social dynamics of the area.

Rural development. An ambitious programme of technical assistance involves more than 1000 rural and indigenous families in the Biosphere Reserve. The programme aims to promote self-sufficiency by helping to develop the production of crops for family consumption. It also aims to increase household incomes by providing technical assistance for cash crop production, by improving key aspects such as productivity, commercialization, and basic community organization.

Education for sustainable development. An environmental and technical boarding school for rural women is run inside the reserve. The school seeks to create real opportunities within the Biosphere area by educating rural women to become truly rural entrepreneurs.

Private initiatives. The Foundation works in partnership with the private sector to further aid efforts to improve the standard of living in the communities where they operate.

Bertoni himself.   School girls going to class.   Planning work on the social and economic development of the area.   Staff of the Moisés Bertoni Foundation providing technical assistance.

IMAGES OF PARAGUAY TODAY

Street market, the Palace in Asunción, oxen transport, old steam railway, traditional *tataqua* earth oven, horses grazing on the Chaco, Berta Roja a great guitarist ambassador for Agustin Barrios Mangore, Asunción station.

IMAGES OF PARAGUAY TODAY

The new Congress, the yellow Lapacho tree, Paraguayan football supporters during the 2010 World Cup, *ñandutí*, harp making and evidence of the harp in Jesuit Reductions engravings.

PARAGUAYAN CUISINE *Rosemary and Robert Munro*

The traditional food of Paraguay has some similarities with the food of the River Plate — *Milanesas* (fried breaded cutlets), *Empanadas* (wrapped bread or pastry with meat or vegetable stuffing) and *Asado* (wood-fired oven grilled meats) are shared with Argentina, Uruguay and other countries — but there the similarities begin to fade and the influence of the ancestral guaranís makes its presence felt.

In Paraguay, *mandioca* (cassava or yuca) and maize are the main supplements of beef and these three ingredients appear in many dishes. Cassava flour, called *almidón* with cheese, eggs and milk are the ingredients of the traditional *Chipa*, a type of bread that should be enjoyed hot at any time of the day, alone or accompanied by a *mate cosido*. Almidón is also the main ingredient of the delicious *mbeju*, a kind of thick pancake that must be eaten immediately after cooking. *Payagua Mascada* is produced by deep-frying a mixture of mince beef with mandioca and herbs.

The *Sopa Paraguaya* (Paraguayan Soup) is not a soup at all, but a savoury cake that looks very much like a sponge cake and is made with cornmeal, whilst *Chipa Guasu* (Big Bread) follows the same recipe but uses fresh corn.

A good *Asado* would consist of at least three different cuts of beef, plus sausages, black pudding and some *menudencias* (livers, kidneys, heart, tripe, and the like). Chicken and pork are served frequently but lamb very rarely. *Asado a la parrilla* is cooked in a barbeque, *asado al asador* is cooked on large wooden skewers and *asado a la olla* is cooked in an iron pot. The *asado* is always accompanied by boiled *mandioca*, *Sopa Paraguaya* and salad.

Puchero is a soup with meat on the bone, vegetables, and maize, *Soo'jo sopy* is a soup made with mince beef and rice, whilst *bori bori de gallina* is a chicken consomé with noodles made of cornmeal and cheese.

Paraguayan food is never spicy but herbs feature in many dishes: coriander, oregano and parsley are used abundantly.

For desserts there is *Mazamorra*, white maize cooked in milk and sugar, *Dulce de Guayaba con Queso*, guava jam with cheese or *Pastafrola*, a pie filled with guava jam. The juice of the sugar cane is called *mosto* and can be drank cold or boiled to produce *Miel Negra* (Black Honey) or *Miel de Caña* which can be served with cheese or made into *dulce de mani*, a sweet bar not unlike brittle, whilst *Pan de Miel* is a cake flavoured with *Miel Negra*.

Fruits are abundant and are normally consumed in season; oranges, pineapples, water melons, papayas, bananas, avocados and mangos can be bought cheaply from street markets everywhere.

Asado a la olla   *Miel Negra*   *Sopa Paraguaya*   *Mbeyu*

Indigenous people do not want to be objects of pity or recipients of charity (although, as in any society, there are always people that will take advantage of what is on offer, praying with the church or supporting the politician that has promised some provisions or the chance of a few days' work). Neither do they want to be seen as some kind of exotic species that should be confined to reserves and protected from the rest of society. Most indigenous people want to share in the benefits of the modern world: they want a good education for their children, health care, transport, mobile phones, internet, TV and global brand names.

They also want their values and cultures to be respected and they want the same rights and opportunities as anyone else. Many indigenous people believe their values, knowledge and understanding of the world are important, not just for their own communities, but for the nation as a whole. The elder generation can remember when much of Paraguay was covered in forest and they had a good diet and the environment was free from pollution. Nowadays the wild animals, birds and fish have become scarce and many communities are confined to small areas of land that are not even sufficient for subsistence farming; people are migrating to the cities and they urgently need to learn new ways to procure their livelihood.

THE INDIGENOUS PEOPLES OF PARAGUAY

John and Graciela Renshaw

Who is and what is Indigenous in present day Paraguay?

There are around 100,000 indigenous people in Paraguay — the Second Census of Indigenous Peoples carried out in 2002 gives a total of 86,540 people — and they comprise less than two percent of the country's total population. It is perhaps surprising that indigenous peoples are so clearly distinguished from the rest of the Paraguayan population, given that Paraguay is the only country in Latin America where the majority of the population speaks an indigenous language. Most Paraguayans believe themselves to be descendants of the inter-relationshiops between the Guaraní and the Spanish *conquistadores* (as well as later immigrants from Europe and the Near East), but they do not consider themselves to be indigenous.

The indigenous peoples of Paraguay on the other hand see themselves first and foremost as belonging to specific ethnic groups or peoples. In fact, it might be valid to ask whether the sense of being "indigenous" rather than say, being Mbyá or Nivaclé or Toba, is something that was born out of the indigenous movements of the 1970s and the Law on Indigenous Peoples (Law 904 of 1981). Nowadays there is no question that Paraguay's indigenous peoples share a sense of common identity that also encompasses the indigenous peoples of neighbouring countries.

The different ethnic groups are distinguished by cultural features: some speak their own languages, others, especially among the Guaraní-speaking peoples, are defined by their mythology and religious beliefs, and typically believe themselves to be the truest, most authentic representatives of the Guaraní. They do not, however, share any sense of political unity. The indigenous peoples of Paraguay are highly egalitarian. There are indigenous political leaders and there are religious leaders and shamans, but their authority is based on their personal qualities and abilities, and their followers are largely drawn from their kin and dependents. In fact, there are almost no formal roles of authority other than the leaders or *Caciques* that have been registered by INDI — the government agency responsible for the welfare of the indigenous people — in accordance with the Law on Indigenous Peoples. These leaders have little or no authority outside their own communities and in fact many indigenous communities have a number of leaders who typically represent the interests of their kin and followers rather than the community as a whole.

Real indigenous leadership is different — and is perhaps a universal quality that comes to the fore in societies that lack formal roles, hierarchy or administrative structures. It is the ability to motivate and inspire, and to take the lead in moments of crisis. A true leader has to embody the qualities of courage, courtesy and self-control. A leader must also be generous; in fact, traditional indigenous leaders were often the poorest people in their communities, as they had to provide for their kin and followers. Nowadays indigenous leaders are more likely to try to satisfy the demands of their communities by lobbying INDI, local governments or NGOs for emergency provisions or "projects", and this has generated a dynamic that is leaving many communities increasingly dependent on outside aid.

Where the indigenous population are located

The indigenous population is divided almost equally between the Chaco and the Eastern Region: the 2002 Census of Indigenous Peoples gives a total of 42,691 indigenous people in the Chaco and 43,849 in the Eastern Region. This means that while indigenous people represent a significant part of the population in the Chaco — 31% out of a total of 138,760, they comprise only a small minority of the population of Eastern Paraguay (0.9% of a population of 5,044,320). In Annex 1 we have included a table that shows the population and location of the different ethnic groups.

The Guaraní: The Guaraní-speaking peoples are found in the Chaco and in Eastern Paraguay. The Guaraní Occidental and Guaraní Ñandevá live in the Central and Northern Chaco; they practise agriculture and some ranching, and many Guaraní men work as builders, drivers or mechanics in the Mennonite Colonies (there are an estimated 30,000 German-speaking Mennonites in Paraguay, about half of whom live in colonies in the Chaco) and in the commercial centre of Mariscal Estigarribia. They take pride in celebrating an annual ritual called Areté Guazú, which is a time of carnival: they dress up in colourful costumes and masks, and sing and dance to celebrate the presence of the spirits (*almas*) of their ancestors among their contemporary kin.

The Aché: In Eastern Paraguay, the Aché, who speak a related but distinct language belonging to the Guaraní linguistic family, were nomadic hunters and gatherers who lived in the dense forests of Eastern Paraguay. Until as recently as the 1970s they were hunted down and many Aché children were captured and sold as servants or foster children (*criados*). Nowadays the Aché live in sedentary communities. Most of their forests have been depleted and they have had to find other ways of subsisting: some have taken up agriculture and others work on ranches and farms.

The Avá, Mbya and Pai Tavytera: In Eastern Paraguay live the Avá, Mbya and Pai Tavytera who speak dialects of Guaraní. The Avá Guaraní used to work in conditions of debt slavery cutting yerba mate or timber; nowadays they get their livliehood mainly from agriculture, with some communities still practising traditional techniques of farming. The Avá Guaraní are an intensely religious people and the older generation maintain their traditional religious practices. However, the Avá Guaraní have found it difficult to remain insulated from the influence of Catholic and evangelical missionaries, and this has led to conflict within Avá communities and in some cases the younger generation has abandoned the traditional rituals. One of the most important Avá Guaraní ceremonies is the children's naming celebration (*Mitakaraí*), which is organized every year, and requires the organisation of prayers and dancing. The Mbyá Guaraní live from hunting, gathering and subsistence agriculture, as well as wage labour for outsiders. Their religion is closely tied to their forest environment, and their religious values are expressed through their prayers, their music and their songs. They believe that happiness is important to maintain the good function of the community. Nowadays the older generation are finding it difficult to maintain their values due to the constant movement of families who travel to the cities, especially to Asunción to seek justice, protection and titles to their land; the children are learning new ways of living, and are missing out on learning about their traditional ways in their own communities. The Paí Tavyterá live in Northeast Paraguay. This is a region of hills and escarpments, and the highest, most dramatic peaks in their traditional habitat form part of a sacred topography, centred on Jasuká Vendá or Cerro Guazú, where they believe the world originated. The Paí Tavyterá have a number of important rituals, especially the boys initiation ceremony, at the end of which the boys' lower lips are pierced.

The Toba Qom: The only Guaicuru-speaking group in Paraguay are the Toba Qom, although there are many Toba and Pilagá in Argentina. They were hunters and gatherers, but have settled and become agriculturalists, ranch hands or wage labourers. The Toba Qom believe in a God called Achen, but in the past forty years evangelical cults have become the norm in the Toba communities, mixing traditional and Christian beliefs. The Toba have a rich mythology, with myths of the origin of women and the adventures of Tanki — the crested caracara, a trickster, who stole fire and killed a monstrous serpent. Dreams are important and Toba shamans interpret their dreams, warning people of diseases that are coming to threaten the community. The Toba still consult shamans about illnesses as well as using modern medicine.

The Enlhet/Enxet: The Lengua Maskoy speaking peoples are found in the Chaco and comprise the Enlhet and Enxet (Lengua Norte and Lengua Sur), the Toba and Toba-Maskoy, the Sanapaná, the Angaite and the Guaná. They speak similar languages and share similar cultures, and often intermarry, so that some people are not sure exactly to which ethnic group they belong. The Enlhet/Enxet are the largest ethnic group: the Enlhet inhabit the area of the Mennonite Colonies and the Enxet live in the Lower Chaco, in the area of the Anglican mission of Makxawaiya. The Toba and Toba Maskoy, Sanapaná, Angaite and Guaná live in the Alto Paraguay, the Central Chaco and to the south and east of the Mennonite Colonies. These people were hunters, gatherers and practised seasonal agriculture, but their lands were sold off in the late 19th Century after the War of the Triple Alliance

(1864-70) and they were forced to work in the logging camps and factories of the tannin companies, such as Carlos Casado, that once dominated the Alto Paraguay, or on the huge ranches that were established in much of the Lower Chaco. Since the 1970s many communities have acquired land, but many Enxet, Sanapaná and Angaite continue to work as ranch hands and some are exceptional riders. Others plant sweet potatoes and squash and keep small herds of cattle or flocks of goats and sheep. These peoples enjoy dancing and playing a drum, which is made from the hollowed trunk of a *caranday* palm covered with a piece of stretched deer hide. The musician beats out a rhythm with a stick and sings, while the dancers dance in a circle around the singer, with their arms linked.

The Ayoreo and Chamacoco: The Zamuco speaking peoples comprise the Ayoreo and the Chamacoco, who are divided into two groups: the Ebitoso and the Tomaraxo. They live in the Department of Alto Paraguay: the Ebitoso are hunters and fishermen who live along the banks of the Paraguay River, while the Tomaraxo used to live in the interior and only recently moved to the river. The Ayoreo lived in the interior of the Chaco and were hunters, who cultivated small plots of maize, beans, squash and watermelon during the wet, summer season. The Ayoreo and Chamacoco are divided into seven clans. Membership of the clan is inherited in the male line and the clans are exogamous, that is to say marriage is prohibited with anyone from the same clan. Both societies have a complex mythology and ritual life. Most rituals — including the Great Ritual of the *Debylyby* (the Chamacoco boys' initiation ceremony), where the adult men wear masks and dress up in elaborate costumes that represent the *Anabsonro*, the Chamacoco deities — were abandoned years ago as a result of pressure from missionaries. In recent years, the Chamacoco have taken a renewed pride in their culture and have started to revive these ceremonies.

The Nivaclé, Lumnanas and Mak'a: The Mataco-Mataguayo speaking peoples: the Nivaclé, Lumnanas (Manjuy) and Mak'a inhabited the area between the Pilcomayo River and what is now the Mennonite Colonies. They were hunters and fishermen, who practised seasonal agriculture and gathered a variety of wild fruits and vegetables, the most important of which were the pods of the algarrobo (carob) tree, which were dried, ground and sifted to make a sweet flour or were steeped in water and fermented to make algarrobo beer. From the beginning of the 20th Century the Nivaclé worked in the cane fields of Northern Argentina, and from the 1950s began to make seasonal migrations to the Central Chaco, where they worked as labourers for the Mennonites. Many Nivaclé settled in the Mennonite Colonies, in the so-called "worker villages" and later in the agricultural colonies set up by the Mennonites. Many Nivaclé believe their traditional values are being threatened by the individualism that is fostered by life in the Mennonite Colonies and some have returned to the area of the Pilcomayo where they have established permanent settlements.

The Lumnanas are a small group; some live in the worker villages in the Central Chaco — where they have intermarried with the Nivaclé; and others live in the Northwest Chaco, where they hunt and work on the ranches. The Mak'a live in the area around Asunción and earn a living selling handicrafts to tourists. They were brought to Asunción by General Belaieff, a Russian émigré, who had employed them as scouts when he was preparing maps of the Chaco for the Paraguayan Army prior to the outbreak of the Chaco War (1932-35). As a reward for their services they were given an island opposite the Botanical Gardens of Asunción, where they lived for many years until the island was abandoned because of flooding. Although they live in close proximity to the city, they have managed to maintain much of their language and culture. ●

ANNEX 1. INDIGENOUS PEOPLES BY LINGUISTIC FAMILY AND ETHNIC GROUP

Language Family and Ethnic Group	Population in the 2002 Census	Region and Departments
TUPI GUARANÍ LANGUAGE FAMILY		
Guaraní Occidental	2,155	Chaco: Boquerón
Guarani Ñandeva	1,984	Chaco: Boquerón
Aché	1,190	Eastern Region: Canindeyú, Caazapá, Caaguazú
Avá Guaraní	13,430	Eastern Region: Canindeyú, Alto Paraná, San Pedro, Caaguazú
Mbyá Guaraní	14,324	Eastern Region: Caaguazú, Caazapá, Itapua, San Pedro, Concepción
Pai Tavytera	13,132	Eastern Region: Amambay, Concepción, Canindeyú
GUAICURU		
Toba (Qom)	1,474	Chaco: Presidente Hayes; Eastern Region: San Pedro
LENGUA MASKOY		
Enlhet/Enxet (Lengua Norte y Sur)	13,065	Chaco: Presidente Hayes, Boquerón
Sanapaná	2,271	Chaco: Presidente Hayes
Toba/Toba Maskoy	2,230	Chaco: Presidente Hayes, Alto Paraguay
Angaite	3,694	Chaco: Presidente Hayes
Guaná	242	Chaco: Alto Paraguay, Presidente Hayes
MATACO MATAGUAYO		
Nivaclé	12,028	Chaco: Boquerón, Presidente Hayes
Mak'a	1,282	Eastern Region: Central (Greater Asunción); Chaco: Presidente Hayes
Lumnanas (Manjuy)	452	Chaco: Boquerón
ZAMUCO		
Ayoreo	2,016	Chaco: Boquerón, Alto Paraguay
Chamacoco (Ebitoso & Tomaraxo)	1,571	Chaco: Alto Paraguay
TOTAL	**86,540**	

EL PANTANAL *Robert Munro*

The Pantanal is the world's largest tropical wetland of any kind. It lies north of Paraguay extending into Mato Grosso, Brazil, as well as into portions of south eastern Bolivia. It covers an area estimated at between 140,000 and 190,000 square kilometers, possibly 3% of the planet's entire wetlands. The name *Pantanal* comes from the Spanish word *pantano*, meaning wetland, bog, swamp or marsh.

There are two distinct seasons in the region: a dry season, from April to September, and a rainy season, from October to March. During the rainy season up to 80% of the Pantanal is submerged under water, nurturing an astonishing biologically diverse collection of aquatic plants and helping to support a dense array of animal species. It is this extensive flooding — sometimes as high as 5 metres — that gives rise to the unique wetland habitats. The Pantanal, like the Amazon Rainforest further north, is an ecosystem which houses a huge variety of fauna and flora including river fish that attract wading birds such as Jabiru storks, snowy egrets and roseate spoonbills.

Like the Amazon rainforest the Pantanal faces the challenge of human incursions and the need to grow crops. Though it is still relatively small, the threat is increasing rapidly particularly in the Brazilian cities located in the higher lands bordering the Pantanal, such as Guaibá. The endless pursuit to satisfy the human need for food poses a serious threat to the fragile equilibrium of the region.

Now is the time to recognise the vital contribution made by this region not only to Paraguay, Bolivia and Brazil, but to the whole world and to introduce measures to preserve and protect this unique and valuable ecosystem.

"Arriving at Tres Gigantes is to relive the story of Creation. Nature lives, and to experience this in person is the most amazing thing I have seen." Fernando Lugo, President of Paraguay

Paraguay has been blessed with a very strategic location: the centre of South America in which many different biomes — major communities of plants and animals with similar life forms and environmental conditions — converge, interact and create "transition zones". This gives the country an amazing variety of life, a great part of which is perhaps still unknown and for those species known, still very much to be understood.

The largest biomes are the Chaco and the Atlantic Forest which run along either side of the Paraguay River and rarely meet. Towards the south of the country, the Pampas grasslands penetrate like fingers into the southernmost areas of the Atlantic Forests and in the north the savannah creates isolated patches of Cerrado habitat. While the Pampas give Paraguay the sensation of never-ending yellow grasslands in a very flat landscape, the Pantanal floodplain and the Humid Chaco provides the same feeling, but with palm trees everywhere. The Atlantic Forest gives Paraguay all the variety of huge, tall rainforests with great biological richness. The Cerrado, very much a savannah-like biome, gives the sensation of a strange habitat with grasslands interspersed with forests prone to catching fire. West of the Paraguay River, the Chaco flows gently in an immense area of broad-barked, green forest, hot and full of oddly-shaped bottle-trees (Palo Borracho) that have been described either as "a green hell" or "a drunken forests". Another biome, the Pantanal, which finds its southernmost point in the very north of the western part of the Chaco, is a huge wetland with perhaps the most important biomass in terms of vegetation and animals. *(see opposite).*

PARAGUAY'S UNIQUE NATURAL ASSETS

Alberto Yanosky

Discovery channels

Paraguay is a natural history "hothouse" waiting to be discovered. In the decade of the 1970s, a species only known to science from fossil records, the Chaco Peccary (*Catagonus wagneri*), was discovered living in the Paraguayan Chaco and well known to the indigenous people. Today with better access to the Chaco the Peccary is relatively easy to spot. The first squirrel in Paraguay was only discovered recently. Three years ago we would have said that we do not have squirrels in Paraguay. Two years ago, two new species of reptiles, a snake and a leg-less lizard were discovered in the Atlantic Forest. And it was in Paraguay that the first ever seen freshwater sponge was found in the waters of the Pantanal. Scientists are still discovering the fantastic natural wealth of the country and it can be firmly said that Paraguay is immensely diverse with much still to be discovered, especially in the Western region, which until recently has been a very inaccessible and harsh environment.

But the undiscovered country, or at least its undiscovered flora and fauna, is also in danger of disappearing before further findings can be made. In recent times Paraguay has seen the destruction of its forests, with the loss of almost all the Atlantic Forest, and now deforestation advances in the Chaco. Agriculture, livestock production, urbanization and infrastructure are the main driving forces which threaten the fauna and flora of the country. The only way to save part of this wealth is knowing it, feeling it and being conscious about what is being lost. What is lost is lost forever, no matter how much we regret those losses. While President Lugo was visiting the Biological Station in Tres Gigantes (Three Giants) in the Pantanal he said "*Arriving at Tres Gigantes is to relive the story of Creation. Nature lives, and to experience this in person is the most amazing thing I have seen. From here, I make this plea, which could become a cry from the wilderness: The conservation of the environment is imperative if humanity truly wants to survive. I thank all those who work behind the scenes everyday to ensure this life for future generations. Thank you, Guyrá Paraguay, for showing me the wonder of nature.*" [1]

The rivers run through it

Paraguay can be described as a huge wetland with two big rivers: the Paraná and Paraguay and a series of medium-sized rivers in Eastern Paraguay such as the Jejui and the Tebicuary. The Paraguay river bisects the country to create two very distinct regions: Eastern Paraguay and Western Paraguay.

Eastern Paraguay has grasslands in the south and rainforest to the north with hills no more than 800 metres high which are covered by high and humid forests within a myriad of ferns, orchids, bromeliads and vines. These forests, usually very bright green, are completely transformed into pink when in August-September the *lapacho* blooms leaving no green leaves on its branches as it becomes completely covered in shiny pink flowers. As soon as one tree finishes blooming, another *lapacho* blooms turning the landscape bright yellow in September-October. Most of visitors flying over Eastern Paraguay and Asunción are surprised by these bright colours in the natural landscape of the country.

The western part of Paraguay or the Chaco is mostly a thorny forest in the west and a scrubby savanna in the east. Hundreds of plant species and types can be found that have adapted to droughts and floods. This area has been little researched, areas such as Chovoreka and Cabrera have little information on their biological richness. While the predominant vegetation formations are xeromorphic, thorny, dry deciduous forests in the Chaco, the visitor is surprised to find a rainforest a few kilometres to the east after crossing the Paraguay River. The main trees in the Dry Chaco are *Aspidosperma quebracho-blanco*, *Ceiba insignis* and *Schinopsis quebracho-colorado*.

---

[1] Since its creation in 1997, Guyrá Paraguay has carried out more 350 biodiversity conservation and sustainable development actions. Guyrá Paraguay is a non-profit, non-governmental organization working for the defense and protection of the biological diversity of Paraguay, organizing community action with the goal of securing representative samples of the natural richness of Paraguay, so that future generations may benefit and appreciate them. Community participation in rural areas of the country is one of our most valuable tools in our work and study of conservation. www.guyra.org.py/ingles

Among the shrubs, various species of *Prosopis*, *Acacia*, *Capparis*, that together with *Ruprechtia triflora* and *Cercidium praecox* are prolific on the soil suitable for forests. In contrast, the sandy grasslands usually known as "campos", (open areas along the ancient riverbeds), are characterised by a savanna-like open woodland with the dominant trees being *Astronium fraxinifolium*, *Schinopsis heterophylla*, *Tabebuia caraiba* and *Jacaranda mimosifolia*. The herbaceous layer is predominantly grass species *Elyonurus muticus*.

In the past, fires, frequently lit by indigenous people, helped to keep the vegetation open, nowadays fires are lit by farmers to get better pastures. During the dry season and because of bad practices of rural management, fires cause loss of nutrients, calcinations and pollution, with severe damage to the environment. Sand dunes in the north-western Chaco are stabilized by natural vegetation; the only place where guanacos, a wild llama, can be found in Paraguay. This topography differs markedly from the flat, sandy "campos" in the Central Chaco, but their savanna-like vegetation is very similar. To the south and east, topographic depressions become more frequent. Here, the trees *Prosopis ruscifolia*, *Calycophyllum multiflorum* and *Bulnesia sarmientoi* indicate the cracking of clay soils. The centre of the seasonal ponds, however, have no woody vegetation but some aquatic plants typical of marsh lands. A grassland with species tolerant to water is represented by *Hemarthria altissima*, *Leersia hexandra* and different species of *Paspalum*, all covering the ground. In the humid Chaco, the vegetation is characterised by a mosaic with the irregular distribution of wetlands. The lower areas are seasonally flooded savannas with a palm (*Copernicia alba*) and grasses, together with papyrus-like *Cyperus* and other vegetation such as *Thalia* and *Juncus*, indicating the presence of water, whereas drier areas typically support a tall *Anadenanthera colubrina* forest.

Living with livestock

In the Oriental Region, the Paraguay River valley resembles very much the other side in the Chaco Area with open swamp-like grasslands and marshes. In this region as well as in the humid Chaco it is very common to see livestock combined with nature. Natural grasslands provide the forage necessary for ranching in this region. The predominantly sandy soils of the central areas of eastern Paraguay once supported a dense forest, rich in the quality and variety of hardwood species (e.g. *Amburana cearensis*, *Aspidosperma polyneuron*, *Pterogyne nitens*, *Peltophorum dubium*) which were progressively cleared with little more than ten per cent remaining. Yerba mate (*Ilex paraguariensis*) and the "coco"-palm (*Acrocomia aculeata*) are two native plants of economic importance. The valleys of the Atlantic Forest, dominated by grasslands are nowadays converted into arable lands with zero-tillage technology. The rich areas resulting from the loss of Atlantic Forest have allowed Paraguay to become a champion in zero-tillage production. The undulating plain of the Alto Paraná valley was also once covered by species-rich subtropical forest, much of which has been converted in recent years to intensive livestock production and arable lands cultivated particularly with soya beans and temperate cereals.

Paraguay's parrots and other abundant bird life

Paraguay has 710 bird species, of which 494 could be found in the Chaco, 390 in the Pantanal, 457 in the Cerrado, 598 in the central eastern forests and 418 in the southern grasslands or pampas. The Atlantic Forest has 549 bird species. Parrots are perhaps the most numerous bird group, with 21 species and of which, the

IMAGES OF PARAGUAY'S FABULOUS NATURAL ASSETS AND DIVERSITY

abundant birdlife, a thriving frog and reptile population, the Atlantic rainforest and the Chaco.

MORE IMAGES OF PARAGUAY'S BIO DIVERSITY

capybaras, alligators, many species of storks and egrets, numerous and diverse parrot populations and the Parque Nacional Teniente Enciso.

Turquoise-fronted Amazon (*Amazona aestiva*) is the most common and very frequently kept as a pet. The large macaws such as the Hyacinth Macaw (*Anodorhynchus hyacinthinus*), the Blue-and-yellow Macaw (*Ara ararauna*), and the Red-and-green Macaw (*Ara chloropterus*), are magnificent birds. Some of them can still be seen flying in Asunción between the "Seminario" and the *Mburuvicha-roga* (The Presidential House). Also the Monk Parakeet is very common and its communal nests are found in rural and urban areas. Humming birds decorate the air with their colours and dancing while visiting the many flowers available, 18 species can be found in Paraguay, the most common is the Glittering-bellied Emerald (*Chlorostilbon aureoventris*), which is commonly found nesting under the rooves of houses. Woopeckers are also abundant, with 21 species in the country, most living in forests and the most spectacular are those red-headed such as the Cream-backed Woodpecker (*Campephilus leucopogon*) in the Chaco or the Robust Woodpecker (*Campephilus robustus*) in the Atlantic Forests.

It is very common to be surprised by the shining yellow colour and the melodious song of the Field Flicker (*Colaptes campestris*) which prefers open areas and nests in termite-hills. Despite different landscapes and climatic conditions, it is surprising how species from two distinct areas (Chaco and Atlantic Forest) show the same aspect with very little differences, as if they were duplicates. The White-fronted Woodpecker (*Melanerpes cactorum*) can be found in the Chaco and the Yellow-fronted Woodpecker (*Melanerpes flavifrons*) in the Atlantic Forest; the Pale-crested Woodpecker (*Celeus lugubris*) in the Chaco and the Blond-crested Woodpecker (*Celeus flavescens*) in the Atlantic Forests. There are tree-creepers, such as the Red-billed Scythebill (*Campylorhamphus trochilirostris*) in the Chaco and Black-billed Scythebill (*Campylorhamphus falcularius*) in the Atlantic Forest. These are not the only fantastic bird species, Paraguay has three species of storks including the giant Jabyru stork (*Jabiru mycteria*), several species of raptors, egrets and ibises, ducks and teals, toucans, trogons, and a whole series of passerines ranging from pale-coloured to bright and multicoloured. Paraguay is a paradise of birds. They are easy to spot and easy to photograph.

Asunción is called the Capital City of Birds with 336 species of bird living there. The Bay of Asunción, one of the natural habitats in the capital city, holds more than 270 bird species and is a stop-over for 25 artic migrant species.

Paraguayans being good musicians have dedicated many songs to the birds of the country, combining legends and myths with reality. The most important and characteristic species of Paraguay is the almost extinct Bell Bird, closely associated with the Atlantic Forest. If the Atlantic Forest is lost, many other species will disappear. The Bell Bird was recently declared Paraguay's National Bird by a law demanded by the people of Paraguay.

Animals aplenty

Paraguay is also home to other important fauna, such as mammals, reptiles, amphibians and fish. Invertebrates are very common and many of them probably still to be discovered as Paraguay has not been extensively researched. There are 174 species of mammals with carnivores being very common, among them the Crab-eating Fox (*Cerdocyon thous*) found close to urban areas. Among foxes, perhaps the Maned Wolf (*Chrysocyon brachyurus*) is the star, a large canine with red colours and a peculiar way of walking. The Bush Dog (*Speothos venaticus*) is another hard to find canine, and another Atlantic Forest dweller. Wild cats still roam Paraguay, especially jaguars, pumas, ocelots, together with raccoons, and otters. The giant otter is another star in the waters of the Rio Negro up in the northern part of the Chaco, in the Pantanal area. Monkeys, deer, rodents, especially the capybara, bats and many other mammals compose the diverse mammal fauna of the country.

Reptiles and amphibians are very common, thanks to a country with such diverse climates and habitats. Almost one hundred snakes have been recorded with a great diversity of colour, especially the Yellow Anaconda (*Eunectes notaeus*), which is fairly common. There are three different species of caimans, and 38 species of lizards. Amphibians are abundant everywhere even inside houses and, especially in wet areas such as bathrooms, their cries are very loud and frequently heard, particularly when it is about to rain or when raining. The many species of frogs and toads call their partners to mate with melodic choruses. A total of 83 species of amphibians have been recorded in Paraguay.

Fish are plentiful in Paraguay. A total of 430 fish species have been recorded, though many still lie waiting to be discovered. Fish are an important food source and trade to local communities, and the species most frequently fished are the Manguruyu catfish (*Zungaro jahu*), the *Golden Dorado*, (*Salminus brasiliensis*), the Sorubim catfish (*Pseudoplatystoma spp.*), among many others.

Many remote areas remain in pristine condition and even in the urban areas, such as Asunción, one can, within minutes, be on the riverside, in the Chaco, in the Atlantic Forest, with a high diversity of plant and animal wildlife beckoning. The only way to understand and love Paraguay is by feeling it, by visiting it and by understanding the strong affinity its people have for Nature.

PARAGUAYAN RAILWAYS *Christopher Scruby*

"It was in 1913 that occurred one of the most important events in the history of Paraguay. It is true that this was in no way connected with politics, presidents or constitutions. All that actually occurred, in fact, was the establishment of the steam ferry across the Alto Parana River, by means of which communication was opened up between the Paraguayan Central Railway and the Argentine North Eastern Railway. But the link was actually of the most momentous order; for it was the last in the lengthy chain by which the inland State of Paraguay for the first time in its history was given a direct road to the sea independent of the watery highway offered by its great river."

So wrote W.H. Koebel in his book *Paraguay* published in 1917; but the history of the Paraguayan railways actually started much earlier. The possibility of building a railroad was first proposed in 1854, during the government of Carlos Antonio López, who hired English engineers to conduct surveys and start building one of the first railways in South America. In 1856 the firm J. & A. Blyth, who were the London agents of the Paraguayan government, proceeded to fulfill an order for locomotives, carriages, rails and all the other equipment necessary for a working railway. The locomotives were designed to run on wood since there was no coal in Paraguay. The construction of the track from the centre of Asunción was in charge of British Engineer George Paddison, hired by the government and between 1857 and 1859 the engineers George Thompson, Enrique Valpi and Percy Burrell were also working on the project. The chosen route out of Asunción went eastwards via Trinidad and Luque, then turning south-east towards Areguá, Pirayú and (much later) to Paraguarí.

The first train service was launched in June 1861. It covered a short distance from the Central Station in Asunción to Trinidad, about 6 miles away. Six months later the track was extended to Luque. This extension was commissioned on December 25th, and according to *El Semanario* it gave cause for great rejoicing to the citizens of Asunción. A transcript from this newspaper reads: *"The locomotives have been functioning from 5.00 am until 12.00 pm. It was necessary to add three more coaches to take the people that were expected on board and they*

came not only to Luque but also to Trinidad. In Luque there were organized games, dances and a masked ball, whilst in Trinidad there were also bullfights". In 1862 the rail tracks were extended to Areguá. When Francisco Solano López inaugurated this train service, he brought to Paraguay the latest technology in communication and transportation, causing an economic revolution in terms of reduced cost and saved time. This only lasted for a short period of time when the War of the Triple Alliance (1864-70) brought an end to Paraguay's days of prosperity in the 19th century as well as to further construction of the railway. During the War, the Central Station in Asunción was used as a hospital. The original name of the Central Station was *Estación San Francisco* as it was situated across the road from the *Plaza San Francisco*. This square was renamed *Plaza Uruguaya* in 1885 to commemorate the return by the Uruguayan government of various artefacts that they had taken from Paraguay at the end of the War of the Triple Alliance. Designed and constructed by the British Architect Alonzo Taylor, the Central Station remains an attractive building because of its architecture and beauty; it is not hard to imagine that it was even more outstanding at the time it was built. In 1863 *El Semanario* stated: *"The construction work in the station is going well, soon the building will be completed and will surely become one of the icons of the city"*.

It was not until many years after the War, in 1887, that construction of the railway beyond Paraguarí recommenced, with stations built between Sapucaí and Félix P. Cardozo. In 1894 a further extension was made as far as Yegros. It was not until 1910 that work began on the final extension of the railway to Encarnación, with some financial backing from the Argentine government. The completion of the line as far as the River Parana in 1913 was a very important development for Paraguay. The steam ferry link across the Parana to Posadas in Argentina meant that there was now an unbroken railway line all the way from Asunción to Buenos Aires for the carriage of passengers and freight, including the export from Paraguay of yerba mate. In 1961 ownership of the railway company passed to the Paraguayan government. Due to lack of investment the railways fell into decay and eventually ceased functioning. Only a small section near Encarnación is still operational in 2010.

For further details about the history and development of the Paraguay Central Railway, see the timeline overleaf.

PARAGUAYAN RAILWAYS: TIMELINE

1856 The government of Carlos A. López makes the first payment of 200,000 pesos for the purchase of railway materials.

1858 The British engineer George Paddison comes to Paraguay, hired by the government to take charge of the project.

1860 The government gives 120,000 pesos to British engineers for construction.

1861 The rail service from Central Station to Trinidad and (in December) to Luque is inaugurated.

1862 The station in Aregua is opened.

1864 The railway tracks are extended to the station in Pirayú, Cerro León.

1865 The train service is suspended due to the War of the Triple Alliance.

1869 The Allied armies dismantles the track that had been destroyed during the war. The wagons and locomotives are taken to Buenos Aires by the Argentine army.

1876 The Paraguayan government authorizes the sale of the railway to Luis Patri, a wealthy Italian cattleman.

1886 The government of Bernardino Caballero buys back the railway and extends the line to Paraguarí and Villarrica. Four new locomotives, 91 carriages for people and freight wagons were bought.

1887 The government of Patricio Escobar authorises the partial sale of the railway to the English company The Paraguay Central Railway Company (P.C.R.C.) or *Ferrocarril Central del Paraguay* (F.C.C.P.).

1894 Four locomotives and eight wagons are purchased for the service.

1907 The government relinquishes its shares, leaving P.C.R.C. as sole owner of the railway.

1908 The American Percival Farquhar buys almost all of P.C.R.C.

1910 The Argentine government subscribes stocks for value of 220,000 pesos to extend the line to Encarnación.

1913 A ferry crossing over the River Parana, joining the cities of Encarnación (Paraguay) and Posadas (Argentina), is inaugurated, providing Paraguay with a direct railway link to Buenos Aires.

1959 It is no longer financially viable for P.C.R.C. to provide a train service; the government is determined to maintain the service.

1961 Agreement is reached for the government to buy the entire railway for £200,000. The Ministry of Public Works takes charge of its administration and starts the legal process to make it into an independent entity.

"It is often said, and not without reason, that the *polca* can only be executed by Paraguayans who have heard it since childhood and carry the rhythm in their heart."

Before the arrival of the European in the Americas, the area now called Paraguay was inhabited by several indigenous groups. The practice of music among those native Paraguayans was associated with the various activities of daily life and developed naturally, without much concern to the "aesthetic". The fire was the centre of community life and around it meals were shared and music sprang up, songs about their relationship with nature and the forces of good and evil.

The role of music among indigenous peoples was identical in the various ethnic groups and simply celebrated the joy of everyday situations: fertility, good harvest, casting out evil spirits and encouragement in overcoming difficulties. There were no designated musicians, and music performance was mixed in with other day-to-day activities.

But their music had, and has, one clearly discernible feature: it lacks formal structure. This becomes evident on first hearing it: Something is "missing" to the Western ear. The musical phrase is repeated without apparent change, reiterated over long periods, and only comes to an end when physical fatigue or boredom sets in. As for musical instruments, in most cases, the natives of Paraguay fashioned them from the materials available in the region. So gourds were turned into rattles, hollow logs into drums, lengths of *tacuara* (bamboo cane) into flutes and so on.

MUSIC IN PARAGUAY

Luis Szarán

Music of the colony

With one notable exception, the early colonial era appears to have been a period of low musical activity. In this period, however, records survive that tell of the formation of what would have been the first orchestra and choir of Asunción in 1545 and the foundation by Father Juan Gabriel Lezcano (who was curate of Asunción), of a school for children where he taught music among other things. The big exception occurred at the beginning of the 17th century, with an event that was destined to have deep, prolonged and widespread effects not just on Paraguay's music but also on its historical, economic, political and cultural development. That was the arrival of the fathers of the Society of Jesus.

Repertoire of the Jesuit Reductions

The history of the Jesuit Reductions (missions) in Paraguay, as the Christians settlements came to be known, constitutes a special chapter in the formation of the Paraguayan identity *(see page 15)* and especially its music.

The missionary activity began in 1609, when the governor Hernando Arias de Saavedra (Hernandarias) asked the Father Provincial to send missionaries to evangelize the Indian. The success of the reductions was swift and surprising. Under a strict system of control, the missions, excelled in developing economic activities, such as cattle farming, agriculture and trade, and achieved an extraordinary level economic and political organization. The Jesuit Missions had their own printing works, musical instrument factories and arts and crafts workshops.

Many of the Jesuit priests that came to Paraguay were excellent musicians. Rodrigo Melgarejo was a cleric and virtuoso musician and became the first music teacher to teach music. Father John Vaisseau, call Vase, arrived from Tournai (Belgium) in 1617 bringing with him a number of musical instruments, as well as a large amount of written music. One of the most celebrated musical missionaries was Father Sepp. His real name was Joseph Von Reineg, a nobleman from the Austrian Tyrol. Another missionary/musician was Martin Schmid, who was also a brilliant architect. He designed and directed the construction of the main temple at the reduction of Chiquitos, in what is now Bolivia. He made musical instruments as well as composing numerous pieces which were part of the missions' musical repertoire. But the most significant figure of all was undoubtedly Domenico Zipoli (1688-1726), born in Prato, near Florence, Italy. The most prominent composer of his time in Rome, organist of the Chiesa del Gesu, he composed many works that were published and appreciated in Europe. He wrote and published his "Sonate d'Intavolature" for organ and keyboard. When still quite young he entered the Jesuit novitiate in order to go as a missionary to the famous reductions of Paraguay. He arrived in South America in 1717, in the same boat as Primoli Giovanni, the famous architect of the reductions. Zipoli was sent to Cordoba (in Argentina) to study philosophy and theology in preparation for ordination. He composed many religious works for large choirs and his music became the most prized at the reductions, with copies being sent to the farthest Jesuit towns.

Over 200 years later, in 1974, during restoration work at the Chiquitos church, the Austrian architect Hans Roth came across more than 10,000 music manuscripts belonging to the repertoire of the reductions, among which are numerous pages with the name of Zipoli and other composers. The finely copied pieces, together with a lot of valuable original instruments and a method for teaching music in the reductions, are now under the care of the Archbishop of Concepción in Bolivia.

The most widely used musical instruments in the reductions were the violin, the harpsichord, the organ, the harp and the guitar. The Jesuit mission of Yapeyú, in what is today modern Argentina, became one of the main centres for the construction of instruments. Organs, harps, violins, keyboards, trumpets, horns and chirimía were all manufactured there.

State-sponsored music

After independence in 1811, Dr. José Gaspar Rodríguez de Francia ruled Paraguay for nearly 30 years. He proclaimed himself Supreme Dictator, imposing a strict system of government, and took drastic measures to ensure the country's independence. He closed the borders to minimize the entry of foreigners into the country and restricted the flow of information. During the Francia dictatorship, popular music (at least in a state-sponsored sense) experienced considerable development and dissemination: military bands were organized in all districts of the capital and in the interior. The government stores sold harp and guitar strings at low prices and documents found at the National Archives in Asunción reveal evidence of the importation of great numbers of musical instruments, sheet music and accessories that were acquired by the state. Also of fundamental importance was the foundation of the School of Military Music in 1817.

Plaintive Paraguayan music

The earliest historical references to the nascent Paraguayan music are found in the first half of the 19th century. The brothers J.P. and W.P. Robertson in their book *"Letters on Paraguay"* speak of a plaintive song sung by Paraguayans which they called *Purahéi Asy* ("singing tearful"). This was the result of the fusion of Spanish music, whose rhythms and melodic turns were assimilated and modified, and the Guaraní text, the first signs of Paraguayan music that subsist to this day with no major variations.

From military to dance music

Between 1840 and 1870 Paraguay was governed by Carlos Antonio, first constitutional President of the Republic, and his son Francisco Solano López who inherited the presidency and led the country during the War of the Triple Alliance until his defeat and death in 1870.

Of great importance in the development of professional musical education was the recruitment of the Frenchman Francisco Sauvageot Dupuis, who arrived in Paraguay in 1853 and lived there until 1861. During that time he trained a generation of young musicians and worked on the formation of military bands.

During the five years of the Triple Alliance War (1865-1870), music played a key role both in maintaining the morale of the troops at the front and in creating an atmosphere of optimism in the capital. Epic music such as *Campamento Cerro Leon* (composer unknown), became popular anthems of Paraguay. In the capital, fashion dances such as *Lancero, Cuadrilla, Contradanza, Palomita*, as well as waltzes, mazurkas and polkas, brought from Europe by Mariscal López's life companion, Elisa Alicia Lynch, were performed in parties often held at the National Club.

Over time many of these dances were adopted by the people, modfied, and incorporated into the repertoire of traditional folk dances of Paraguay. Of these there survive today the *Contradanza*, the *Cuadrilla*, the *Lancero*, the *Santa Fe*, *La Golondrina*, the *Montonero*, the *Polca Paraguaya*, the *Londón Karape*, *Palomita*, *el Solito*, the *Cielito*, the *Mazurka*, the *Chotis* (from Schottis) and others. The only surviving dance of indigenous origin is the *Pishesheshe* (*pie arrastrado*).

1874 saw the arrival in Paraguay of the Italian Luis Cavedagni. Baritone, composer and bandleader, Cavedagni is responsible for the earliest printed edition of Paraguayan music. His *"Album de los Toques mas Populares del Paraguay"*, published in 1887, constitutes the earliest record of music and dances of Paraguay: *Palomita, Raido Terere, Cerro Leon, Londón Karape, Colorado, Mama Kumanda, Taita Mandi'o* and more.

Centurion and the new century

The early part of the 20th century was a politically turbulent period in Paraguay, but the outbreak of the First World War brought economic development to the region and witnessed the premiere of the first Paraguayan *Zarzuela* (from the Spanish spoken-sung national theatre): "*Tierra Guarani*", with lyrics by Fermin Dominguez and music by Nicolino Pellegrini.

In this period the country saw the arrival of many foreign music teachers who were responsible for the formation of the first generation of Paraguayan musicians that transcended national borders. Among them was Fernando Centurion (1886-1938), violinist and composer, who trained at the conservatories of Liège and Paris. In 1911 Centurion formed the Haydn Quartet and founded the Gimnasio Paraguayo, a music school. As a composer he wrote the first symphonic works: *Marcha Eroica para Orquesta, Serenata Guarani y Capricho sobre un Tema Paraguayo*. To this generation also belong classical guitarist Gustavo Sosa Escalada and pianist Aristobulo (Nonon) Dominguez, who in 1928 published the most important collection of Paraguayan popular music transcribed for piano: *Aires Tipicos Paraguayos*.

Paraguayan polca

Paraguayan popular music has emerged from the melée of various ethnic components swirling about after the arrival of the first Spanish and European settlers. The national music form was born from the ingenuity of "criollos" who managed to create a musical language with distinctive characteristics. The most widespread form of Paraguayan music is called Polca, which in turn presents numerous variants maintaining similar rhythmic pattern: The *Gallopa*, the *Kyre'ÿ*, the *Cancion* and the *Danza Paraguaya*. The rhythm of the *Paraguayan polca* is not the same as the original Bohemian Polka, which was very fashionable in Paraguay towards the middle of the 19th century. The *Polca Paraguaya* takes nothing more than the name from the Polka and the term tends to refer to music in general. It is often said, and not without reason, that the *polca* can only be executed by Paraguayans who have heard it since childhood and carry the rhythm in their heart.

The first reference to the *polca* as the music of Paraguay was published in the national newspaper "*El Semanario*" on 27th November 1858, in an article about a housewarming party at Venancio López's new house: "*En medio del campo llamado Hospital, había una banda de música militar destinada exclusivamente para diversión del pueblo,que bailó sus cuadrillas, sus polcas y mazurkas al compás de esta ruidosa orquesta …*"

Many of the oldest *polcas* are anonymous: "*Campamento Cerro Leon*", "*Mama Kumanda*", "*Takemi nde pohéi*", "*Alfonso Loma*", "*Pajaro Campana*" and others. Among the best known polcas by registered authors are: "*Maerapa reikuase*" by Rogelio Recalde, "*Tres de Mayo*" by Juan Alarcon, "*Che tromp Arasa*" by Herminio. Giménez, "*Minero Sapukai*" by Emilio Bigi, "*Gallito Cantor*" by Jose Asunción Flores, "*Cascada*" by Digno Garcial and others.

The *Cancion* is a slow *polca* with the same rhythmic characteristics. As in all forms of popular Paraguayan music it is directly influenced by Spanish music. The lyrics are frequently in Guaraní, being the sole contribution of native culture, but even in these cases, the pace of the verses is in Western metric, losing the essence of the Guaraní musical tradition which was not symmetrical originally, but free-structured. Some of the best known tunes of this genre are: "*Asunción*" by Federico Riera, "*Recuerdos de Ypacaraí*" by Demetrio Ortiz, "*Asi Canta mi Patria*" by Florentin Gimenez, "*Reservist Purahéi*" by Agustin Barboza, "*Oracion a mi Amada*" by Mauricio Cardozo Ocampo, "*Paraguay*" by Emilio Bigi, "*Cerro Cora*" by Herminio Gimenez, "*Mi Dicha Lejana*" by Emigdio Ayala Baez and others.

The *Guarania* is a form of Paraguayan music created by home-grown musician and composer José Asunción Flores in 1925. The creator wanted to find a music form that expressed the character of the name Paraguay beyond what was done by the *polca* and its derivatives. He developed a combination of slow rhythms and melodies, sometimes melancholic and sometimes of heroic character, and the *guarania* immediately became for Paraguayan music the most significant phenomenon in the 20th century. From the first creations: "*Jejuí*", "*Kerasy*" and "*Arribeño Resay*", the genre enjoyed extraordinary acceptance, and very soon many composers had adopted the *guarania* as a form of musical expression.

Paraguayan music today

From 1940 Paraguay suffered the loss of many artists and intellectuals, who, under persecution by dictatorial regimes, emigrated to live and work in neighbouring countries. Many of the best composers and musicians such as the aforementioned José Asunción Flores, creator of the *Guarania*, Herminio Gimenez, Carlos Lara Bareiro and others took up residence in Buenos Aires and from there a parallel Paraguayan musical culture developed outside Paraguay.

Meantime, in Paraguay musical activities continue to evolve with Remberto Gimenez, founder of the Asunción Symphonic Orchestra (OSCA) Juan Carlos Moreno Gonzalez, creator of the Paraguayan *Zarzuela*, Luis Cañete, Florentin Gimenez and many others.

Musical activity intensified in the 1970s, especially in the fields of folk and urban music with the appearance of the *Avanzada*, created by Oscar Nelson Safuan in an attempt to modernise Paraguayan popular music, and the *Nuevo Cancionero*, inspired by similar movements elsewhere in Latin America. Both movements, with distinct artistic agendas, managed to create in the last two decades new, unique musical avenues, now incorporated into the true classic Paraguayan repertoire. Much of that repertoire remains umbilically linked to the guitar and Paraguyan harp (*see also pages 66 and 73*).

ABOUT THE PARAGUAYAN HARP *Robert and Rosemary Munro*

Paraguayan culture emerged from the interbreeding of Spanish and Guaraní people, and Paraguayan music is an artistic expression of that emerging culture developed deep in the heart of South America. The Spanish brought with them guitars, harps and other traditional musical instruments. During the 16th and 17th centuries, the Jesuits used music to evangelize the people and showed them how to make and play musical instruments, resulting in today's rich examples of Paraguayan craftsmanship and musical expression *(see also page 61)*.

Of all the musical instruments it is the harp that has become the icon of Parguayan music. Over the years, the Paraguayan harp has become established as the national instrument of Paraguay. Its distinct construction, style and performance techniques have been passed down from generation to generation and have been refined to make it a more sophisticated instrument.

The harp's construction

It stands about 1.5 metres (5 ft) high and is very light and portable. The sound box is made of cedro (a type of mahogany) and pine. It is played either in a sitting position, or standing up when it is fitted with extending legs, using the fingernails as well as the finger pads. The harp has 36 or 37 strings, which pass through the centre of the neck making it identical from either side, this being a unique characteristic of the Paraguayan harp. The lower strings were once made from the leather of the belly of horses, and the upper strings of steel, but now they are all made of nylon. The original wooden tuning pegs have mostly been replaced by machine heads like those on the guitar, making the strings easier to tune.

Harp-making (along with guitar-making) is a craft industry and it is possible to visit the small private factories in and around Asunción. Several are found on the way to Asunción Airport and in the town of Luque, from where Paraguayan harps are exported all over the world.

Playing the instrument

The harp has no pedals and is a diatonic instrument, which limits much of the traditional music to a major key and its related minor. There are however several methods of making accidentals. One is to shorten a string at the lower end by pushing it against a small peg placed between the strings. Another method is to shorten the strings at the top end by means of a metal key which is held between the fingers. More recently, harps have begun to be constructed with the addition of levers to overcome this limitation, and many players are now using levered harps. Arpeggios, glissandi, chords in octaves, thirds, sixths, and other effects are readily executed on these harps. There are sounds unique to the Paraguayan harp, which are produced by damping the strings in different ways or sometimes almost strumming them like a guitar. Also, the beautiful *trino* (tremolo) technique is often played using the fingernails of the dominant hand to bring out the melody.

The two best-known rhythms are the *polca* (or *galopa*) and the *guarania*. Although there is a vast repertoire of Paraguayan music, very little was written down until recent years. Most of the harpists develop their own arrangements and many are masters of improvisation. Most professional Paraguayan players have learnt initially by ear and use techniques never written down in theory books.

One of the greatest and best known Paraguayan harpists was Feliz Perez Cardozo, who died in 1952. He is the composer of some favourite tunes like *Tren Lechero*, *Mi Despedida*, and many others. He is credited with the ingenious arrangement of *Pajaro Campana*, one of the oldest and best-known folk songs of Paraguay. Digno Garcia is another great composer who was inspired by a waterfall to compose the popular piece *Cascada*. Other famous composers are Luis Bordon, Lorenzo Leguizamon, Enrique Samaniego and Nicolas Caballero.

New techniques are being developed and a new generation of composers are creating new styles and sounds for the Paraguayan harp with new pieces that are very different from the traditional polcas and guaranias and there are many brilliant Paraguayan harpists whose talent is now being recognised.

YERBA MATE *Robert Munro*

Yerba mate is a type of tea and the national drink of Paraguay. It is made from the leaves of a species of the holly family (Aquifoliaceae) native to Paraguay which is now also cultivated in northeastern Agentina, Bolivia and southern Brazil. It was first scientifically classified as *Ilex paraguariensis* by Swiss botanist Moisés Bertoni, who settled in Paraguay in 1895 (see box on page 40). At the time of the arrival of the Europeans to the Americas, *yerba mate* was already consumed by the native inhabitants of Paraguay and mate subsequently became the obligatory infusions of the inhabitants of the whole southern cone of South America. During the colonial period it was Paraguay's main export and the Jesuit Missions became major producers. Production and export of *yerba mate*, sometimes referred to as the *Oro Verde del Paraguay* (the 'green gold of Paraguay'), became a state monopoly during Dr. Francia's government (1811-70) and its trade made Paraguay a very wealthy country. After the War of the Triple Alliance (1864-70) the industry fell into the hands of large foreign corporations, mainly Argentinian and Brazilian.

The infusion called mate is prepared by steeping dry leaves and twigs of *yerba mate* into a hollow gourd and adding hot water. Paraguayans however, prefer *tereré*, made with cold or icy water to which a number of aromatic and medicinal herbs are added. Drinking *tereré* with friends, using a shared special straw called a *bombilla*, is a common social practice in Paraguay which transcends age, class or social status. A toasted version of *mate*, known as *mate cocido* is consumed instead of coffee or tea for breakfast or drank throughout the day is small cups similar to expresso coffee. *Yerba mate* is now also available in tea bags to be drunk in a similar way to tea, and in aluminium cans as a fizzy drink.

CURING YERBA.

"A people is as their land and their air is." Gertrude Stein

"Yet when we look beyond this world's unrest,
More miserable then the oppressors than the oppressed"

Robert Southey: *A Tale of Paraguay' Canto III VII*

"Una noche tibia nos conocimos
junto al lago azul de Ipacaraí,
tú cantabas triste por el camino
viejas melodías en guaraní."

Zulema de Mirkin/Demetrio Ortiz *Recuerdos de Ypacarai*
[One balmy night, by the blue waters of Lake Ypacarai, we met.
As you made your way along the road, you sang. Your songs were
sad, ancient melodies, in Guarani.]

PARAGUAY: A PERSONAL PERSPECTIVE

Matt Holland

Almost five hundred years ago and a quarter of a century after Columbus made his landfall discovery, the first explorers to sail from the Iberian peninsula across the Atlantic Ocean, down the coast of South America and a thousand kilometres inland up the River Plate, made their own amazing discovery. They came across a land that was paradisal. Its rivers were full of fish, its fruit always in season, its wildlife wonderful, and its people friendly. They may not have found gold or other precious minerals, but had found something even more valuable. They wrote letters home saying 'This land is wonderful. We may not come home!' In fact, many did not. Instead, they stayed, and colonised the country. This land was Paraguay.

Four hundred years later, another group of life's explorers also discovered the delights of Paraguay, and its difficulties too. They were called the Bruderhof and comprised a few hundred northern Europeans, who were trying to live out the Sermon on the Mount, follow the Christian ideal, calling one another brother and sister, living in community, and aiming to "have all things in common". They lived on small farms in southern England. Their stand against armed conflict meant that, in the 1940s, they had to find a new home, somewhere in the world that was not part of the war in Europe.

They chose Paraguay, which was not at war, had fertile but inexpensive land for sale, and a history of welcoming strangers. The Bruderhof sent an advance party of "strong young members" to hack a home out of the jungle. Once trees had been felled, wells dug, and simple dwellings built, families followed. In 1953, our family, comprising Austrian nurse and Mum Gerty, London artist and Dad Leslie, one baby girl, and five boisterous boys, boarded the *Highland Princess* and sailed, third class, across the ocean blue.

Three weeks later we disembarked in Montevideo, and took a river boat upstream to Asunción. From there, we boarded another ancient bark which chugged further up river to Puerto Rosario. There, we were met by Bruderhof Brothers, known by Paraguayans as *Los Barbudos,* the bearded ones. Along a bumpy red dirt road, in horse-drawn carts, they took us 50 kilometres deep into the Paraguayan campo.

My personal Paraguayan adventure had begun…

Wild boys in a wonderful land

Within weeks, I was a happy barefoot six-year old, the red earth of Paraguay between my toes and the bit of a of a boy-gaucho's life between my teeth. Hot and humming, fertile and fecund, teeming with the stuff of sub-tropical outdoor life, Paraguay pulled me in, to its dangers and delights, in a way that cold old England, damp and decidedly danger-free, had not.

Gone were the days of dragging myself out of bed into a freezing bathroom, trying to find clothes that would keep out the cold, searching for socks, gloves, and wellies, and setting off on a foggy walk to school, passing farm workers trying to start frozen tractors and pitch-forking stinking silage to sleepy black and white Friesian cows. Now, in paradisal Paraguay, we leapt out of bed before dawn, slipped on short-sleeved cotton shirts and shorts, ran out to feed the backyard bantams, watched the cowboys ride their horses bareback across the open campo to round up the sleek wild-eyed Zebu cattle, and then made our sunny way to school, comparing catapults along the way, looking out for snakes in the sand, and scaring screeching paraqueets out of paraiso trees.

By midday, we were done with spelling, history, and maths. What mattered now was to get home, get a bite to eat, and get out on our horses, ride down to the river, go for a swim, climb a tree or three, and look for the stuff of life. The campo, tajamares, swamps, and bosques of Paraguay were ours for exploring.

What Columbus and the conquistadors had done on a continental scale, we were doing on a local one. But we were not looking for slaves or gold. We were watchers, stalkers, and sometimes hunters, of all things natural: fish and cayman from the rivers and swamps, armadillos, parrots, and pigeons from the jungle, as well as wild bees and birds' nests high up in magnificent liana-hung trees, and all manner of snakes and spiders from their secret holes. We were wild boys in a wonderful land.

Every turn we took, Paraguay offered us its natural delights. Blessed by Nature, Paraguay's blessings were available to us, in daily and plentiful supply. Its colours, sights, smells, and sounds were a feast for the senses. And didn't we feast!

Our final and perhaps most significant year in Paraguay, was spent living in a settlement of 500 indigenous people, the Lengua, in the Chaco, north of the great river, an area commonly referred to as the Green Hell.

Well, it was more like Heaven for me. Here, for one wonderful year, school passed me by and the Lengua, the gauchos, and the Paraguayans took me in. They taught me to ride, really ride, on working horses, lively and light on their feet, that responded to neck rein and whispered commands. Knee-deep in swamp, I learned how to spear eels and hook mud fish. Working with my father in a tiny simple supplies store, I learned how to trade flour and sugar for feathers and skins; and how to do all this in the cleverly compound, beautifully onomatopoeic and perfectly pictorial language of the local people, Guaraní and Lengua. Rice was *holiapkapkapuk*, literally, "little white ants eggs".

And then there was the music, a Paraguayan staple. It seemed like every gaucho had a store of songs and stories, that told of love, longed-for, found, and lost. Taking tea (actually *terere*) at regular intervals during the day, passing round the cow's horn *guampa*, and sharing the same *bombilla*, was always an opportunity to connect, to talk about things and reflect on life. Though not at school, this was one 12 year-old who was getting an education all right, in Paraguay.

The splendour of this land-locked country, that sits on the Tropic of Capricorn in the heart of South America, was getting into my blood and bones, in a way that would never leave me. It has informed me ever since.

Even though we came back to England, and I had to get used to keeping warm and dry and wearing a blazer and tie at Grammar School, thoughts of Paraguay never left me. More than 30 years later, I returned, picked up where I'd left off, with cultural and physical adventures too, and now have 'a second home' and circle of friends in Belén, Concepción, Asunción, and elsewhere in Paraguay. Thanks to these connections, it has been possible to create and foster a cultural and meaningful exchange between Paraguay and England, involving in particular Lower Shaw Farm, the Swindon Festival of Literature, Fundacion Libre, Guyrá Paraguay, El Roble, Pablito y Miriam, and Sonidos de la Tierra, with harpists, guitarists, singers, storytellers, writers, gauchos, environmentalists, and all.

As an old Paraguayan songs says, once you dip your toe in the waters of the river Tapiracuai, or the Ypané, you will return, as you do to one you love. And I did. You can come too!

CHACO-I *Robert Munro*

In the days before the bridge crossing the Paraguay River was built 25 kilometres upriver at Remanso, Chaco-i was the gateway to the Chaco. The bulk of the goods destined for the estancias, cities and colonies in the Chaco was transported by launch to Chaco-i and then by road to various points in the Chaco. The Bridge was completed in 1978 and since then Chaco-i has lost its strategic importance.

Chaco-i means 'little Chaco' in Guaraní. It is best reached by launch from Playa Montevideo, just behind the Presidential Palace in Asunción. The ten minutes crossing of the Paraguay River takes you to a magical world. A wilderness where time stands still. Chaco-i is a micro-eco-system supporting a rich variety of fauna and flora. It could become the Everglades of Paraguay. When visiting Chaco-i it is better to take a local guide. Gustavo Britez, who was born and lived all his life in Chaco-i, is one such guide: he owns a launch and his intimate knowledge of the place is invaluable.

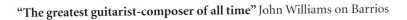

"The greatest guitarist-composer of all time" John Williams on Barrios

Paraguay has produced several figures of international stature in the Arts such as Luis Alberto del Paraná, Augusto Roa Bastos and José Asunción Flores. However, by 2011, none had attained the heights of international acclaim of the guitarist-composer Agustín Barrios Mangoré (also known as Agustín Pío Barrios). Barrios is a unique figure in the 200 years of Paraguayan national cultural history. A musician of universal genius, he died on 7th August, 1944 in obscurity far from Paraguay, leaving scattered throughout Latin America a body of work with a breadth, beauty and sophistication beyond that of any other composer for the guitar before or since. This unappreciated genius was only re-discovered in the West some 30 years later with a release by John Williams of an entire recording of music by Barrios.

AGUSTÍN BARRIOS MANGORÉ:

PARAGUAY'S PRE-EMINENT GUITARIST-COMPOSER

Nicholas Regan

The Paraguayan

Agustín Pío Barrios Ferreira was born on 5th May, 1885 in the rural Department of Misiones in south-eastern Paraguay. His upbringing was not typical for the time and place. While geographically distant from the cultural centres of the time, the Barrios household was nevertheless a highly cultured one. His father was the Argentinian vice-consul, and his mother was a schoolteacher; visits to the home by educated family acquaintances were frequent.

One of these visitors, and the man whose influence on the adolescent Agustín proved crucial, was the Paraguayan-Argentinian guitarist, journalist and businessman, Gustavo Sosa Escalada. Greatly impressed by Agustín's skill on the guitar, Sosa gave him what were to be the only formal guitar lessons that he ever received. It was on Sosa's recommendation that the boy was sent, at the age of fourteen, to attend high school in Asunción. On leaving school in 1902 Barrios continued to teach himself the guitar, studied musical theory under the Italian violinist Nicolino Pellegrini, and also mixed with leading intellectuals of the day. This combination of influences produced a unique artistic and professional vision.

The Panamerican

The principal feature of Barrios' career was his almost incessant travelling. He lived and performed in seventeen Latin American countries, as well as the Caribbean and Europe. The odyssey of this troubadour's life saw him in the company of heads of state, applauded as a genius, and yet at other times hounded by destitution and chronic illness. His nomadic existence began in 1910 when he left Paraguay, initially for a two-week tour, and did not return for twelve years. However, despite his apparent wanderlust, it was a dejected Barrios who reluctantly left Paraguay in 1925 for the last time. His request to the government for permission to set up a Guitar Conservatory in Asunción had been declined: although he was a well-known musician locally, his political affiliation may have limited Barrios' ambition inside Paraguay. A few years later, finding himself obliged to cancel concerts in Buenos Aires through declining public interest, the disillusioned Barrios finally took the decision in 1929 to abandon the River Plate region altogether, never to return.

New name, new success

A profound change then appeared in his professional persona. Around 1930 Barrios adopted the stage name of Nitsuga Mangoré: Nitsuga is simply Agustín spelled backwards, but Mangoré is, significantly, the name of a legendary Guaraní chief, who died for love. He took to appearing in concert dressed in 'Indian' regalia, including feathers and bare chest, and billing himself as 'The Prodigious Guaraní Guitarist', and 'The Paganini of the Guitar from the Jungles of Paraguay'. It may be that Barrios had calculated that he would attract a larger audience by pandering in caricature to prevailing stereotypes of Paraguay. An alternative possibility is that his own analysis of his artistic worth may have led him to re-define himself as an artist identified with the indigenous heritage of the Americas. This alignment would make Barrios one of the first South American artists to present himself as an artist overtly of the New World, while simultaneously observing Old World levels of musical sophistication.

Whatever is the case, the newly branded Chief Nitsuga Mangoré now began to enjoy unqualified success. In Venezuela he played over thirty concerts in two months during 1932, a feat seldom equalled, if at all, to this day by concert guitarists. As he pushed north through Central America to Mexico in 1933, he befriended the Paraguayan Ambassador, Tomás Salomoni. He persuaded Mangoré to leave behind the character of Chief Nitsuga, and was responsible for fulfilling Barrios' cherished dream of visiting Europe. It was not to be a concert tour — in the 15 months that Barrios and his wife were with the Salomonis in the Old World, Barrios gave only a handful of small recitals — but the experience must have been profound. In 1935 Paraguay's own bloody conflict with Bolivia over the Chaco region occupied the League of Nations in Geneva. Nazism was on the rise in Germany. Civil war in Spain was approaching, and the world was spiralling towards World War Two. On his return to Central America in 1936, Barrios' perennially poor health deteriorated further, and in 1939 he all but ceased performing, settling in El Salvador to devote himself to teaching. He died there, virtually ignored, in 1944.

The maestro's legacy

The works of Barrios Mangoré are universally admired for their exceptional beauty and outstanding intensity. The majority of them contain attractive melodies but are deceptively complex in structure and enormously demanding on the performer. His musical style corresponds, as might be expected, to the main facets of his own identity, namely classically trained, raised in a rural town, and a bohemian. He transcribed and performed works by Bach and Beethoven. In almost all the countries that he visited he composed concert works based on local indigenous styles, absorbing forms as diverse as the Argentinian zamba, the Caribbean zapateado and the Chilean cueca; and he developed remarkably lyrical waltzes and barcaroles for the guitar.

In almost all contemporary reviews of Barrios' concerts, reference is made to his extraordinary virtuosity. Though largely self-taught, he not only acquired a refined range of contemporary technique, but extended the technical possibilities of the classical guitar. He was, notably, the first classical guitarist to make commercial recordings. The 40-plus discs that he cut between 1913 and 1929 reveal not only the wealth of his work and his technical mastery of the guitar, but the fact that Barrios believed absolutely in the guitar as a serious concert instrument, and in his own music as a worthy competitor to any other of his age.

From obscurity to celebrity

Far away from the eyes of the Eurocentric classical guitar world, interest in Agustín Barrios remained alive through the mid twentieth century in Uruguay, Venezuela and El Salvador. However, it was in Barrios' homeland that the first of the two critical events occurred that were to trigger global recognition of his genius. In 1953, the Paraguayan government of Federico Chávez commissioned the guitarist Cayo Sila Godoy and the novelist Augusto Roa Bastos to travel through Latin America to compile the works of Barrios for the nation. Sila Godoy continued this task for the next 50 years, eventually amassing the collection of recordings, photographs and manuscripts that would go on public exhibition in Asunción in 2007.

The second pivotal moment catapulted Barrios suddenly to the attention of the international classical guitar arena. This was the release in 1977 of the LP *John Williams Plays the Music of Barrios*. Williams shares the credit for the spectacular rescue of Barrios from obscurity with the ex-students of the maestro himself who were still living in El Salvador. In 1969 they entrusted Carlos Payés, a student travelling to Spain to take up postgraduate studies, with the task of seeking out the world's foremost guitarist, John Williams. Payés duly met Williams after a concert in Madrid and asked if he would consider looking at the Barrios manuscripts in his possession. Swept away by the quality, variety and quantity — some 50 pieces — of the music he found himself reading, Williams declared Barrios 'the greatest guitarist-composer of all time', and the classical guitar world greeted Barrios as a lost treasure. The Paraguayan genius had finally found his way to a global concert audience, by the most unlikely of means, yet in the most capable of hands.

The legacy of Barrios

In life Barrios was a cultural exile: early 20th-century Paraguayan musical society was not equipped to support a talent of his magnitude. Even after his death, through the 1950s and beyond, the national government did not approach its own emissary, Sila Godoy, to bring to the public the archive he had so carefully gathered. A major investigative biography of Barrios was not published until 1992, and only then by a North American researcher. Nonetheless, by 2011 important progress had been made in securing the legacy of Barrios: the Guzmán Museum in San Salvador was established as the Central American focal point for devotees of Barrios, and from 2007 the unique Sila Godoy collection was finally put on public view at the Cabildo Museum in Asunción. Meanwhile, a portion of Barrios' manuscript music remained lost. The collection of his recordings was incomplete, and biographical data was unreliable, riddled with hearsay and personal opinion. What little documentation Barrios' low-key career had generated was destroyed or allowed to decay over the years. (Several collections of Barrios-related material were still being kept from public view by their guardians.)

In death, Agustín Barrios Mangoré had indisputably achieved the recognition that eluded him during his life. His works were on the 2011 syllabus of almost every guitar conservatory in the world. His own recordings were broadcast in 2010 for the first time since 1935 on BBC Radio 4 in London. The world of classical music marvelled at the wealth of his oeuvre, and the Paraguayan government had finally come to recognise and value his legacy.

In 2009 the Paraguayan government of President Fernando Lugo requested the repatriation of Barrios' remains, the most recent of several requests, yet one that El Salvador once again declined, fuelling the continuing dispute over each country's entitlement to the heritage of Agustín Barrios Mangoré. The Salvadorian stance was that whereas successive Paraguayan governments failed to embrace Barrios, right up to the beginning of the 21st century, by contrast in life he had been welcomed and celebrated in El Salvador. The government of President Maximiliano Hernández offered Barrios a post in the National Conservatory when he ceased touring and he chose to live out his days there. Paraguay, meanwhile, maintained its de facto claim to the mortal remains of a Paraguayan citizen and what it now considers a major figure in its cultural heritage.

As the Barrios phenomenon continued to gain momentum in 2011, the paradox of his life became ever more poignant. With a tireless tour schedule lasting over 30 years, remarkable technical ability, and a musical output unparalleled by any other guitarist in the world, it is ironic that, while unrecognised in Latin America, and unknown to North American or European critics, the guitarist-composer Agustín Barrios Mangoré surpassed in all respects the rivals of his time, and remains unrivalled to the present day. ●

The country has honoured Barrios by placing his image on the new 50,000 Guaranies notes.

"The destruction of the originals or first versions is part of my working method... I prefer to start with complete freedom in front of a blank paper, which is my great tyrant."
Augusto Roa Bastos

Augusto Roa Bastos, who was born in Iturbe on 13th June, 1917, was a writer whose words have penetrated Paraguayan history and culture very deeply. His famous phrase *"Paraguay is an island surrounded by land"* accurately describes the country's isolation now and probably for many generations to come. The fact that he was forced to live most of his life in exile, or — as he preferred to put it — 'in seclusion', seemed to have given him a special insight into who we are, because while trying to find himself as a writer, he also discovered (or uncovered) our true nature.

"I prefer to talk about a painful absence rather than exile. Exile was an atypical, strange university for me. It allowed me to learn about things that I wouldn't have known otherwise". He told me this shortly after publishing *El Fiscal* (1994), the third of his trilogy of novels inspired by Paraguay's series of despotic and "embracing" — as he described them — absolute rulers. The other novels in this collection are *Hijo de Hombre* (1960) and *Yo, El Supremo* (1974).

His masterpiece, is undoubtly *Yo, El Supremo*, a first person account of the life of Gaspar Rodríguez de Francia. The narrative becomes so vivid and the story so real that by the end of the book readers feel deeply confused about whether they are actually reading the dictator's own memoirs. At the end of the story there is an epilogue, where Roa Bastos refers to himself as a *"compiler"* and pretends to quote Francia himself, saying: *"It is not necessary to know the origins; to learn that those fabulous stories are not from the time they were written. There is a deep difference between a book written by an individual that is presented to the public and one that is written by the public. You cannot doubt them that this book is as old as the people who dictated it. The story in these notes explains the story that should have been written but has not been told. Therefore, characters and facts have won, by the fatality of a written text, the right to an autonomous and fictitious existence, at the reader's service"*.

AUGUSTO ROA BASTOS:
BRINGING PARAGUAYAN HISTORY TO LIFE WITH WORDS

Andrea Machain

The constant inspiration from history

Augusto Roa Bastos navigates easily in history without having being an academic historian. He always made it clear that although his stories may have taken inspiration from history his work has never been historical. *"All my books are literary fiction. They are not history books. I have previously researched history extensively but I never wanted to mix the two. So they are not history books as some seem to believe. Historical references are the prime source material that I processed completely to transform them into almost pure works of fiction".*

Each work of Augusto Roa Bastos seems to have been written by a different person as each of them is unique. "*I never wanted to have my own style; I thought it was important for every work to have its own language*". He was known to destroy entire manuscripts when he was not completely satisfied with the results and start from scratch. "*The destruction of the originals or first versions is part of my working method. I have difficulties in taking notes or in recycling fragments of work so I prefer to start with complete freedom in front of a blank paper, which is my great tyrant*".

For a man who spent almost half of his life outside his country, returning to the land that inspired most of his work was a difficult experience: "The emotional shock of coming back to the country after so many years of exile was like two strangers who took a while to recognize each other. I had to learn again about a country that after such a long time was different from my own vision". Part of the distress was having to admit what a long dictatorship had done to the country: "*A degradation caused by so many years of absolute power is similar to the erosion suffered by nature, in a process that I call social ecology.*"

'Writing' wrongs

He dedicated the last years of his life to counter this degradation, giving free talks and lectures to students and supporting several education initiatives for adults. He also kept writing, always with great realism, as if he could never depart from or completely cast aside his earlier profession of journalist and screenwriter. After serving a short period in the army during the Chaco War (1932-1935), he travelled to Europe where he worked as a war correspondent, including a brief spell at the BBC headquarters in London. Back in Buenos Aires, as a professional screenwriter, he wrote several scripts for Armando Bo and his wife Isabel Sarli, for the celebrated B movies based on some of Roa Bastos tales.

This constant inspiration from history continued until late in life. In 2001 he wrote an imaginary dialogue between the Argentine painter Cándido López and General Bartolomé Mitre [statesman, author, and President of Argentina 1862-68]. that took him into deeper philosophical grounds: "*Tutela tu tela mirando con un ojo el pasado y con el otro, el recuerdo. No reconocerás al uno en el espejo del otro. Ya ves, este paisaje de sangre parece un mal sueño. ¿Y qué importa si está al revés o al través? Lo que importa es el recuerdo que tendrá el porvenir. La memoria del pueblo que mira desde adelante para atrás. Todo se puede mejorar siempre, maestre. El arte es el arma para corregir la realidad.*"

Even before the publication of *Yo, el Supremo*, Roa Bastos had already established himself as a significant literary figure, due to *Hijo de Hombre*. However, *Yo, el Supremo* consolidated his place in the pantheon of great writers. Carlos Fuentes has described *Yo, el Supremo* as one of the milestones in Latin American literature. While his reputation rests on his novels, Roa Bastos' achievements in film, creative writing, and journalism add further substance to his legacy. He died in Asunción on 26th April, 2005, aged 87. ●

ÑANDUTÍ LACE: *Jennifer Baldock*

Ñandutí (Guaraní for spider's web) is the Paraguayan lace made by weaving fine cotton thread with a sewing needle on a light cotton cloth stretched over a wooden frame. This is a typical Paraguayan handicraft developed particularly in Itagua and Pirayú, south east of Asunción. The first mention about local women making *ñandutí* is found in *Letters on Paraguay* by J.P. and W.P. Robertson published in London in 1838.

Ñanduti is very similar to the sun lace (because of the rays stemming from a centre) from Tenerife in the Canary Islands. It is similar also to the Spanish sun lace that originated from the needle lace and bolillo lace from Arabia. The itinerary it followed was: Arabia to Spain to the Canary Islands to the Southern Brazilian Coastline and the River Plate to Paraguay, resulting in what is today known as *ñandutí*.

Suns and frames are the designs that predominate in *ñandutí* lace, to which the Paraguayan women add their own creations inspired by objects around them such as flowers, plants, and animals. There are said to be over 100 basic patterns which are put into the compositions according to the weaver's fancy. The design, which is created by each artisan, is made up of suns and trimmings. The areas that remain between each sun are covered with a stitch called *arasapé*.

Once the piece of *ñandutí* is finished the cloth behind the lace is cut away, leaving the outer part that is attached to the frame. The lace is then washed and starched and once dried is removed from the frame and the remaining cloth.

All white, ochre, multicoloured or of a single colour, the lace is made into several sizes of doilies, place mats, tablecloths, stoles, mantillas, altar cloths, and the like. Some modern Paraguayan couturiers have incorporated *ñandutí* into elegant evening gowns, wedding dresses and other fashionable items.

CRAFTS *Rosemary and Robert Munro*

The arts and crafts of Paraguay are beautiful. In addition to the traditional ñandutí lace, mainly produced in Itaguá, gold and silver filigree, pottery, leather goods, wood carvings and sculpture, wool and cotton weaving are produced by artisans all over the country.

Located about 20 kilometres from Asunción the City of Luque has produce many artists, poets, writer and musicians, as well as one of the best football teams in the country. The silversmiths of Luque produce beautiful filigree jewellery in gold and silver in their rudimentary workshops located around the central square.

El poncho de sesenta listas (sixty stripes poncho) has been produced for almost 200 years. The Marisca López (1826-70) often wore one when riding. In Piribebuy, Rosa Segovia, who learned the craft from her mother and grandmother, is now herself training 12 young girls on the complex weaving designs and techniques. The poncho is made using fine cotton thread on a very simple loom and it takes one weaver six weeks to complete one.

A distinctive style of pottery is found in Itá, about 35 kilometres east of Asunción where beautiful and ornate items are made using the local black clay. Among the many potters, Rosa Britez is singled out for her originality and the quality of her work. A prolific worker, she has been named *Ceramista de America* and has exhibited in Korea, France, Germany, Spain, Mexico, the USA and all over South America.

The women of Santa María de Fe, one of the 30 pueblos founded by Jesuit missionaries in the 16th and 17th century, make some of the most beautiful hand-sewn craftwork in the country. Over a period of more than 20 years, a group of about 25 women of the *Taller de Hermandad* (Workshop of Sisterhood) have been producing this appliqué craftwork, showing traditional scenes from peasant life.

Indigenous arts and crafts are sold in the streets of Asunción by Maká people. Always ready to be photographed (for a small fee, mind you) these ancestral Paraguayans sometimes still appear slightly confused and bewildered by modern Paraguay. They proudly cling on to their inheritance, passing on their culture and traditions from generation to generation.

Rosa Britez, *la Ceramista de America*, works a lump of clay into a pot without using a wheel. This ability comes from her native ancestors as seen below, taken in 1911.

Rosa Segovia at her *tellar* weaves a *poncho de sesenta listas*.

Freedom is a contradictory word in Paraguayan history. It depends on who defines it, how it is defined and in what context. For instance, the so called "father of journalism", Don Carlos Antonio López, the Paraguayan leader who followed the long dictatorship of Dr. Francia, was during his period in office also editor of the first newspaper in the country, *El Paraguayo Independiente*. There is clearly a contradiction between being the editor of the only newspaper and at the same time being the non-elected political leader, who also wrote the first Paraguayan constitution which states that nobody can be the owner of a printing company without receiving permission from the "Supreme Government".

Free speech and the freedom of the press evolved slowly throughout Paraguayan history. In the last two decades (1989-2009) some educated people linked democracy with the possibility of making these two important human rights key elements in building a political process which gives people full access to opportunities. Some recent local and international polls have shown just how disenchanted people are with democracy. Paraguay is, according to the Chilean pollsters Latinobarómetro, one of the countries least enthusiastic about democracy. Almost 50% of the population is ready to give up some freedoms in exchange for better economic and social conditions. This demonstrates the deep impact that the long dictatorship of General Alfredo Stroessner (1954-1989) had on education in Paraguay.

Education, free speech and freedom of the press

It is difficult to appreciate freedom of the press and freedom of speech in a country where investment in education during the Stroessner regime was 1% of GNP (Gross National Product) and in the democratic period has just reached 2.8% of GNP. This is far lower than in Uruguay, Costa Rica or Chile where people view democracy with enthusiasm and hope as a means of building a strong state based upon the rule of law. There is a clear link between education, free speech and the freedom of the press.

BETWEEN SILENT TRADITION AND NOISY DEMOCRACY

Benjamín Fernández Bogado

The level of illiteracy is still high. The government speaks of a level of about 10%, but in reality it is over 45%. This makes it difficult to enjoy freedom of speech and the freedom of the press. The present Constitution drafted in 1992 says these freedoms are to be enjoyed with responsibility, equity and veracity. Newspaper circulation is very low for a country with more than six million people. Less than 130,000 copies are distributed from the capital city, Asunción. *ABC Color*, the most popular newspaper, sells 20,000 copies daily whereas in 1984, before it was closed down for five years by the Stroessner regime, sales reached 80,000. This large fall in circulation at a time of increasing population is proof of disenchantment with the press. Many people see the press as more interested in confrontation and dispute with the political establishment than in helping the people participate in the democratic process with knowledge and information. Some recent polls also show that even though people are disenchanted with the executive, legislative and judicial institutions of democracy, they still trust the media and the Catholic Church. Nevertheless, there has been a big drop in that trust compared to just after the overthrow of Stroessner in 1989 when people held journalists and the media in high esteem.

Lack of formal education, untrustworthy media and the very small distribution of newspapers and books are key factors in understanding why free speech and freedom of the press did not play a more important role in creating enthusiasm for democracy. From a legal point of view the current Paraguayan Constitution drafted in 1992 is one of the most advanced in the region in terms of protecting freedom of speech and the freedom of the press. It authorizes public access to information and protects both these freedoms. Articles 24 to 29 repeat the importance of the freedom of expression and the freedom of the press in strengthening democracy and human values. The Paraguayan constitution is used as a model in Latin America as regards fully protecting free speech and freedom of the press. It protects the interests of citizens as well as those of journalists, photographers and media owners. It clearly precludes governments from closing newspapers and magazines and shutting down radio or television stations because they disturb the political establishment. There are also some important advances in the criminal code even though one can be sued under the criminal code rather than the civil code for libel cases. This argument was used by some political figures against journalists who dared to publish articles on corruption. Judicial decisions show that in some cases judges consider the interests of politicians to be more important than the interests of individuals in cases where journalists decided to publish articles covering corruption, which is still a big problem in Paraguay. Annual reviews by Transparency International still list Paraguay as one of the most corrupt countries in Latin America. The popular perception is that corruption is still very high due to lack of convictions against corrupt public servants. Impunity is high in Paraguay where people who commit a crime have a 99% possibility of not being prosecuted, fined or sent to prison. This situation makes journalists dispair of reporting cases of corruption, because they see their work as useless and without any support from the judiciary. Also this situation makes people say: "Under democracy we can say whatever we like, but nothing happens when we complain. With democracy we can talk, but we cannot afford to eat."

The internet: beyond the censorship control?

New technologies have started to play an important role in building a more participatory civic society. The internet reached Paraguay in 1997, but even now only 10% of the population has access to it. The number of users is, however, increasing among the young. Some civic programmes are pushing for more access to the internet and teaching how to use it. *Fundacion LIBRE* with its CETICOM (*Centro Tecnológico de Información y Communicación*) teaches how to use new technologies in order to develop media on the internet. Since its first courses, many people have started their own blogs and spread the idea of the importance of new technologies for developing the freedom of the press and free speech. Much remains to be done in this field which could be a very important factor in encouraging a sense of power to publish ideas without fear of censorship or control.

Fear has played an important role throughout Paraguayan history. A major social evolution took place following the arrival of democracy in 1989. People are no longer afraid of expressing ideas, but lack of education makes it very difficult for them to hold serious discussions on diverse issues. This situation can be observed by listening to Congress debating on sundry important matters. Lack of cogent argument gives people a sense of disappointment regarding the importance of freedom of speech and democracy. Personal attacks among congressmen are normal and serious debates are very rare.

Words fail them...

Another important element which plays a sensitive role is the bilingual characteristic of Paraguay. People speak Guaraní and Spanish. About 60% of the population speaks only Guaraní, whereas Spanish is the language of commerce and politics. This situation restricts fluency in the expression of ideas when discussing diverse issues. There is a long way to go in order to make Paraguay a fully bi-lingual country where people can comfortably express ideas in both languages with confidence. The state is beginning to teach people in Guaraní and use Spanish as a second language, but the results after almost 20 years of implementation are poor due to a shortage of teachers with a good command of both Guaraní and Spanish.

Freedom of speech and the freedom of the press require the encouragement of reading in order to give people the vocabulary and the ideas necessary to participate in conversation and discussion. Guillermo Jaime Etcheverry, a former Rector of the largest Public University in Argentina, Universidad de Buenos Aires (UBA), wrote in his book "*La Tragedia Educativa*" that a young student in Buenos Aires uses less than 300 words to communicate daily, whereas the Spanish language has more than 100,000 words. If this is the situation in a city where people speak more than any other place in Latin America, one can imagine how many words are used in Paraguay.

Another statistic shows that young people in Paraguay read less than 25 pages of a book in a year. Cost is not a real problem because books normally cost only $5 US. Lack of a public library system is also a problem. In 2009, the director of the National Public Library, the most important one in Paraguay, resigned because she had not received any salary for nearly five months. The lack of encouragement of reading and low interest by the official authorities in implementing public policies to stimulate reading have tragically resulted in people being poorly qualified to exercise free speech and benefit from the freedom of the press.

Paraguay's silent society needs to speak clearly and articulate ideas

It is necessary to find a solution to this problem in order to make people aware of the importance of both freedoms in developing their own personality and to enjoy the advantages of these freedoms. People admire those who are able to speak clearly and articulate ideas, but there are insufficient places to learn these skills. The Secretary of Education must promote this sensitive and important issue of strengthening personality. It is common to note in social discussion that many people want to participate with ideas and concepts on different issues. However, they are not able and free to participate because they are ashamed to express their ideas as they are not trained to do so. It is rare to find Paraguayan families where members express their ideas freely over lunch or dinner. The authoritarian tradition permeated every part of society making silence and self restriction part of the national culture. Paraguay can be defined in many ways as a silent society where there is still social control on people who want to express their own ideas in school or social gatherings. Perhaps, rhetoric needs to be taught again in state schools.

Education is vital

To conclude, it is not sufficient to merely enshrine freedom of speech and freedom of the press in the Constitution. We Paraguayans need to understand that it is necessary to build a social consensus on the importance of both freedoms in a country which suffered for so long from censorship, fear and the persecution of ideas. It is necessary to reduce inequality in education and improve access to new technologies, but at the same time it is important to promote reading, publications and access to public libraries in order to give people the tools to enjoy freedom of speech and the freedom of the press.

Paraguay has experienced a long tradition of silence in its two hundred years of independence. Presently, the country is enjoying more than 20 years of democracy. However, the impact of past censorship upon the population is clear to see. Probably, the biggest impact is seen in education, which can have the most positive effect on democracy and the overall understanding of freedom.

"In his death and the extermination of his nation, Solano López achieved a triumph far greater than the victors; a triumph achieved at the cost of innumerable defeats, of abominable terrors, of an abominable pride, of an abominable holocaust." **Augusto Roa Bastos, in El Fiscal, 1993**

Portrait of Don Carlos Antonio López c.1845.

A statue of Mariscal Francisco Solano López (1826-70) — Don Carlos's eldest son and the essence of *paraguayidad*. His name, even in defeat, is forever linked to the independent nation of Paraguay.

A SPECIAL DAY *Gloria Morel*

On August 1st 2004, news shocked the nation that a fast-spreading fire had killed 420 people. Victims of the inferno in a crowded supermarket on the outskirts of Asunción found that locked doors blocked their escape. This is one survivor's personal account …

Sunday 1st August 2004 was a special day in Paraguay. It was the last day of the *Semana de la Amistad* (Friendship Week). The temperature forecasted for the day was a minimum of 12°C and a max of 20°C, fresh with cloudless skies. A beautiful day. I was preparing to attend the religious service at Comunidad Cristiana de Asunción on Artigas Avenue when I was told that the grandmother of a dear friend had died: that meant rearranging my day to enable me to be with my friend at the wake. I took the short walk from home to the Comunidad Cristiana Church and on the way I passed the historic *Iglesia de la Santísima Trinidad* where a mass was being celebrated. I paused to admire the imposing architectural structure dating from the 19th Century. I arrived at the service at 9.15am ready to worship God and thank him for his love and mercies while sharing in the communion service.

At 11.00am I decided to leave before the end of the service. My day was full with a host of activities organised and I was keen to pay a visit to my friend who had just lost her grandmother. On the spur of the moment I decided to enter the *Supermercado Ycua Bolaños* situated 80 metres away from the church to buy coffee and sugar for the wake. The *Supermercado Ycua Bolaños* was built in 2001 and opened on 7th December that year. So it was exactly 938 days old. It was a monumental building covering 8,340 square metres with a car park at ground level and the supermarket above, accessed by two ramps located at each end of the building. It was fully air-conditioned and the ceiling was made of polystyrene tiles to keep the cool air in.

On entering the building I left my Bible in the left luggage box and walked in. I was wearing a red jumper and a leather jacket. I collected coffee and sugar and made my way to one of the express tills as I only had two items to pay for. The girl at the till was named Gloria, like me, and as she handed back my credit card we heard an explosion.. "Sounds like a terrorist attack" I said. "Oh, it is just problems in the kitchens" — she said — "It happens from time to time".

The author outside and inside the supermercado.

PAGE **85**

As I walked away from the till I was knocked down to the ground by a mass of people running, who trampled me down. As I tried to crawl out of their way I heard what sounded like machine gun fire and saw the ceiling in flames collapsing on top of us. The lights went out and I realised I was in the middle of a major fire. I took refuge under a counter and prayed. I could see the flames turning people into human torches.

The apocalyptic scene reminded me of a horror movie. Soon an eerie silence took hold of the place. I could not hear a human sound and thought I was the only survivor. Then I heard hammering noises from outside and knew I had to make a move. I covered my face with my leather jacket and started to walk in the dark looking for an exit. I realised I was walking over charred bodies. I heard voices and walked towards them, I raised my hand and felt I was being lifted up above them. I found myself in the hands of a fireman who immediately passed me into the hands of another and then a third. A fourth fireman laid me on a stretcher. I remember nothing else.

Postscript *Gloria was taken to hospital at IPS* (Instituto the Prevision Social) *about a mile from the place of the fire, where she spent 2 hours. She was then transferred to* Centro Medico Bautista *where she spent 60 days, followed by many months of rehabilitation. She returned to work in February 2005. Her full story is told in her book:* Estoy Viva para Contar *(Dacol: 2005)*

• *The* Cruzada Mundial de la Amistad *was founded by Dr. Ramon Artemio Bracho and a group of friends on 20th July 1958 in Puerto Pinasco a small town about 300 miles north of Asunción on the River Paraguay. The* Día Mundial de la Amistad *(World Friendship Day), 30th July, is faithfully celebrated in Paraguay every year and has been adopted in several other countries.*

• *The voluntary firemen of Paraguay came of age during the* Ycua Bolaños *fire. This gallant body of men and women, teenagers many of them, fought the fire, rescued the injured and dealt with the gruesome task of lifting the charred remains of over 400 victims who died on that day. They are organised in two separate groups: the* Cuerpo de Bomberos Voluntarios del Paraguay *(known as the* Amarillos*), founded in 1978 and the* Junta Nacional de Cuerpos de Bomberos Voluntarios del Paraguay *(known as the Azules), founded in 1980. Now covering most of the country, the brigades are composed entirely of volunteers, most of them in university education, many holding full time jobs. Fiercely competitive and incredibly proud of their own "colour", they faithfully toil for no reward but the honour of serving. And honour them we do.*

Simulation exercise for fireman today in Asuncion.

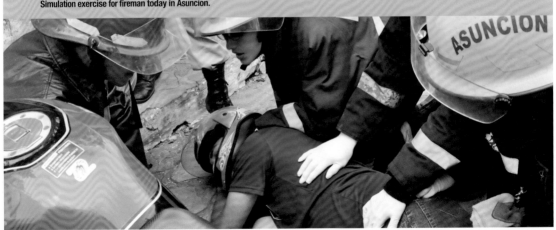

> **"It was not until President Lugo was elected to the presidency in 2008 that for the first time in Paraguayan history a political party replaced another in a democratic election."**

Paraguay has changed out of all recognition in the two centuries since its independence in 1811 and yet some deep-rooted cultural features provide an enduring link with the past. Even the territory of what we define as Paraguay has altered considerably as a result of the country's involvement in two major wars. In 1811 the independence leaders of Paraguay had laid claim to significant areas of what is today Argentina and Brazil. Both of these powerful neighbours refused to even recognize Paraguayan independence until many decades later. By 1911 Paraguay's defeat in the Triple Alliance War (1864-70) had stripped it of roughly one-fifth of its pre-war territory — land comprising part of the modern-day Province of Misiones, Argentina and the State of Matto Grosso, Brazil. The simmering dispute between Paraguay and Bolivia concerning possession of the enormous Chaco region worsened over the subsequent decades and was finally resolved with Paraguayan victory over Bolivia in the Chaco War (1932-5). So by 2011 the definitive borders of the country had been established, giving it ownership of most of the Chaco Boreal, which now comprises 61% of the total area of the country.

CHANGE AND CONTINUITY IN PARAGUAYAN HISTORY:
1811, 1911, 2011

Andrew Nickson

Population see-saw

Many of the dramatic changes in Paraguay's history have been driven by rapid population growth. On the eve of independence the estimated population in what is today Paraguay was no more than 110,000 and most people lived in small rural settlements within a 50-kilometre radius of the capital, Asunción, which had a population of only 7,000. By 1911 the total population has risen to around 600,000, much less than would have been the case had the country not suffered the genocidal effects of the Triple Alliance War, which decimated the population. A recent major study calculated that the population fell from around 420,000-450,000 in 1864 to around 140,000-166,000 in 1870. This represents a loss of 60 to 69% of the pre-war population, far higher even than previous estimates. Recuperation was slow until

basic health care was finally extended into rural areas during the second half of the 20th century. As a result, the population growth rate rocketed from the 1960s, nearly tripling in the 40 years from 1972 (2.3m) to 2011 (6.7m).

Waves of immigrants

The aftermath of the Triple Alliance War saw the inflow of a sizeable immigrant population from Western Europe, especially Spain and Italy. Although on a much-reduced scale compared to that in neighbouring Argentina and

Brazil, by 1911 most urban centres had sizeable communities of first generation European immigrants. The 1930s saw the arrival of new migratory flows — Mennonites, fleeing from Russia via China and Canada, followed by eastern Europeans from Poland and Ukraine in the 1940s and 1950s. Immigration of East Asian peoples started from Japan in the 1950s, followed by Koreans and Chinese in the 1960s and 1970s. But the most sizeable immigrant flow, beginning in the 1970s, came from neighbouring Brazil, comprising the so-called brasiguayos, commercial soybean farmers of second-generation Germanic and Slavic extraction. So by 2011 Paraguay had become a far more ethnically heterogeneous and cosmopolitan country than it was in 1911, a phenomenon personified by 31-year old Yolanda Park, one of the country's top TV presenters, whose parents are Korean.

The explosive population growth continued to pose an enormous challenge to Paraguay. Today the population is 60 times greater than it was in 1811. By contrast, the population of England and Wales had grown from 10.6m in 1811 to 54.5 in 2011, only a fivefold population increase. Yet in the United Kingdom these two centuries witnessed a dramatic economic transformation wrought by industrialisation, and was thereby capable of providing a majority of jobs in the non-agricultural sectors of the economy. By contrast, one of the perennial features of the Paraguayan economy over the past 200 years has been the continued dependence on agriculture as the mainstay of the economy and employment. The only exception was the incipient manufacturing that took place during the short period of state-led development (1840-65) initiated by President Carlos Antonio López prior to the Triple Alliance War, and to which over 300 skilled British contract workers made a significant contribution.

Paraguay's primary products

At independence, foreign trade was virtually confined to the export of yerba mate tea, hides and tobacco. By 1911 there had been considerable diversification of exports, into cotton, sugar, tannin extract, timber and corned beef, much of which was produced by a British company, Liebigs. During the second half of the 20th century the agricultural economy underwent a radical transformation as virtually all of these crops and products were replaced by soybean and chilled/frozen meat produced by commercial farmers and modern cattle-ranchers. In the process, the area under agricultural and intensive cattle production expanded rapidly, forcing a growing migration of under-employed school-leavers to urban areas and, more recently, into economic exile. By 2011, 810,000 young people, 48% of all those aged between 15 and 29, were either unemployed or underemployed.

One striking feature of this evolution of the economy is that in 2011 Paraguay has remained as reliant on the export of 'primary products' as it had been in 1911 and 1811. Despite the massive 7,000 MW of electricity generating capacity from its joint ownership with Brazil of the Itaipú hydro-electric plant, Paraguay has not experienced any energy-intensive industrialisation process in the period after 1980 when the first turbines came on stream. The failure to use the country's energy resource to electrify the railway system has also contributed to a dramatic shift in inland goods and passenger transport. From 1909, two years before the centenary of independence, the British-owned Paraguay Central Railway reached the border town of Encarnación, a distance of 441 kilometres. Its service from Asunción to Encarnación was of far greater economic importance than the hazardous alternative by road, especially after inter-connection was made with the Argentine railway system in 1913. Yet by 2011 a triangle of highways linked Asunción, Encarnación and Ciudad del Este and the railway only operated a small section near Encarnación. *(See also box on 'Paraguayan Railways' page 58)*

All-embracing agriculture = destructive deforestation

The over-reliance on agriculture and the associated expansion of the agricultural frontier has decimated the dense forest that once flourished in most of Paraguay. In 2011 less than 2% of the semi-tropical 'Atlantic' forest that previously covered much of eastern Paraguay remained. In the decade up to 2011 an even more rapid process deforestation began to take place in the Chaco, at an average rate of 2,500 acres per day. In both parts of the country the destruction of the natural environment has been led by brasiguayo soybean farmers, encouraged by weak enforcement of Paraguay's environmental protection laws. As a result the visual landscape of the country has altered out of all recognition over the past 200 years. This is most striking in the Departments of Alto Paraná and Itapúa, which extend to the Brazilian and Argentine borders respectively. In 1911, the indentured labourers who picked and carried yerba mate on their backs were called 'miners' precisely because they used lamps to guide themselves through the dense forests. In 2011 this region of the country now resembled the flat plains of the mid-western states of the United States.

Hydro-electric potential

While forest cover is fast disappearing, Paraguay's other great natural resource — the Paraguay-Paraná river system — is making a greater contribution to economic development. The tapping of the enormous hydro-energy potential of the Paraná basin has led to the development of the Itaipú and Yacyretá hydro-electric plants with Brazil and Argentina respectively. Until the Three Gorges hydro project in the Peoples Republic of China is completed, Itaipú remains, at 14,000MW, the largest hydro plant in the world. In the process of its construction, the majestic Guairá waterfalls, a hitherto emblematic feature of the country, visible yet inaccessible in 1911, disappeared under water when the lake behind Itaipú dam was filled. A new canal and lock system around both hydro plants, together with extensive dredging, have greatly increased commercial transport on the Paraná and Paraguay Rivers and by 2011 the bulk of Paraguay's soybean and other grain exports were transported on enormous barge convoys to the River Plate. *(See also box on 'Hydroelectric Power' page 33)*

Society on the move

The rapid population expansion and associated migration to urban areas has also put strains on the capacity of the state to provide basic services to its citizens. However, despite the difficulties, the educational and health profile of Paraguayans has improved markedly over the past century. Educational enrolment in 1911 was little more than 10 % of the primary school age population. By contrast, in 2011 Paraguay had achieved universal primary education, although completion rates for secondary school remain far below the Latin American average because of a high drop-out rate. In 1912 the Universidad Nacional (founded in 1889) was the only university in the country, with only 116 registered students, the vast majority studying law. By 2011 there were 49 recognised universities and the number of enrolled university students was around 150,000.

There has been a similar improvement in the basic health profile of the population as a result of the expansion of public health services and disease control programmes. In 1911 malaria, tuberculosis and hookworm were still endemic in rural areas, with leishmaniasis and leprosy still common illnesses. Poor diet and living conditions contributed to a low life expectancy which was worsened by the virtual absence of doctors in rural areas. The infant mortality rate (under one year of age) had fallen from around 80 per thousand live births in 1960 to around 20 per 1,000 live births in 2011. However, the maternal mortality rate was still far above the Latin American average due to the limited coverage of MCH (Maternal and Child Health) programmes in rural areas.

The exclusionary nature of Paraguayan society

In spite of these improvements in the delivery of basic health and education, the culture of the public administration system in 2011 continued to reflect the exclusionary nature of Paraguayan society inherited from the past. This was built on an extremely unequal system of land tenure, which remained little changed throughout most of the 20th century. In the absence of a merit-based system of recruitment and promotion, patronage and nepotism continued to strongly influence the inner workings of ministries and public sector bodies. Although a targeted anti-poverty programme in the poorest departments of San Pedro and Caazapá got off the ground from 2006, public sector workers, especially in the judiciary, continued to display negative attitudes towards the poor majority that were surprisingly similar to views reported from a century earlier.

Efforts to bring the state closer to the citizen have been very slow in Paraguay. Even the basic parameters of citizenship were very slow to evolve. It was not until 1914, three years after the centenary of independence, that a law was passed extending the registration of births and deaths by the State, the *registro civil*, from Asunción to include the rest of the country. Although a semblance of local government already existed in 1911, with 72 municipalities, it was only in 1991 that municipal mayors were elected by citizens for the first time — prior to that they were all appointed by the President of the Republic. Judicial reform has been similarly slow and treatment of the rural poor by the judicial system remains grossly inadequate despite the construction of six brand new Court Buildings throughout the country during the 1990s. Legal redress for the poor remains an illusion as they continue to be at the mercy of unscrupulous lawyers, in a fashion also not dissimilar to 100 years ago.

Coup and counter coup

This continuity in the gross weaknesses of the public administration system is not surprising when viewed against the limited democratisation that has characterised most of Paraguay's life as an independent nation. Despite the much vaunted 'liberalism' prevalent in 1911, politics remained the preserve of a tiny majority, who settled their differences by coup and counter-coup rather than appealing to the democratic wishes of the people. Numbers on the electoral register were tiny in relation to the size of the adult population. Recourse to the mass of the population was primarily for cannon fodder at times of armed conflict. In fact, for 100 years from 1911 to 2011 there were no less than 20 occasions on which the government changed as a result of a military-led coup, as well as countless more failed coups. It was not until President Lugo was elected to the presidency in 2008 that for the first time in Paraguayan history a political party replaced another in a democratic election.

Cultural clues to Paraguayan identity

It is noteworthy that Paraguayan culture has demonstrated great resilience in spite of enormous structural changes in the country over the past two centuries. Popular religiosity remains strong although the influence of the Catholic Church has diminished considerably. While in 1911 over 96% of the population were nominally Catholic, the actual presence of the church was already extremely limited in rural areas, and became increasingly dependent on foreign-born priests and nuns. By 2011 a growing presence, within rural and urban communities, of missionaries from the evangelical branch of the Protestant Church, Mormons and Jehovah Witnesses has reduced the proportion of nominal Catholics to little more than 75% of the population.

Culturally isolated for many decades before and during the Stroessner dictatorship, the "island surrounded by land" (as Augusto Roa Bastos famously described Paraguay) opened rapidly to the outside world during the decade prior to the bicentenary under the influence of the global IT revolution. 'Foreign' cultural influences have clearly gathered strength. Cachaca and cumbia have replaced the polca and the guarania as the preferred music and dance of young people. Yet unlike virtually anywhere else in Latin America, most people in Paraguay still speak an indigenous language — Guaraní. Indeed, the most striking example of the strength and identity of Paraguayan culture is this endurance of the national language in the everyday lives of Paraguayans.

Still a common tongue?

Most significantly, there is little evidence of a decline in Guaraní usage despite the rapid rural-to-urban migration that has taken place since the 1980s. The census (2002) showed that Guaraní was still the favored language in Paraguay, preferred by 59 percent of households compared with 36 percent of households that preferred Spanish. A further 5 percent of households spoke other languages, mainly Portuguese, German, and Korean. In rural areas, Guaraní remained by far the predominant language, preferred by 83 percent of the population, and more households there spoke other languages (8.9%) than spoke Spanish (8.4%).

Yet the national language has endured in spite of the extreme hostility towards it shown by the Paraguayan elite and the state throughout almost all the nation's 200-year history. In 1911 it was still officially prohibited to speak Guaraní in schools, a situation that did not really come to end until the 1960s [1]. Even in 2011, the Paraguayan state, with rare exceptions, does not communicate with its citizens in the national language. Medical students at the Universidad Nacional are not required to pass an exam in Guaraní as part of their training, in the judicial system there is no provision for defendants to give evidence in Guaraní, and Guaraní still does not even figure on the passport of Paraguayan citizens. This contradictory attitude towards Guaraní — at one and the same time praising it as "the embodiment of Paraguayan identity", while at the same time showing disdain for Guaraní speakers — is at the heart of the complex belief system that maintains an exclusionary style of development.

---

[1] A striking example of the elite disdain for guaraní appears in the postscript to the major commemorative album sponsored by the Paraguayan government on the first centenary of independence in 1911: *"As for the removal from the national education system of Guaraní, that dialect or archaic indigenous language which serves no purpose whatsoever, it only remains to carry this out, as a crucial first step in our enormous campaign. Yes, sir! To completely de-Guaranize 'in order to ensure that the roots of that primitive forest do not regain their control in the open furrows' and then to crisscross the land everywhere with railway lines, in order to spill out European immigration in every direction, in the struggle for its expansion."* (Monte Domecq' 1911, author's translation)

Towards the next centenary

Many of the problems facing Paraguay can be traced to this exclusionary style of development that has characterised the country's history during the first 200 years of its independent life — the limited nature of democracy, the gross inequalities in income and land tenure, the venality of many powerful politicians and administrators, and the disdainful attitude toward the poor and marginalised groups. Indeed, the challenge of the next century will be for Paraguay's leaders to break with this tradition and promote a genuinely inclusive style of development in which the poor majority are allowed to play a more important role in the economy. With the necessary political will and a massive investment in high quality public education, there is no reason why richly-endowed Paraguay should not be able to provide a sustainable and decent standard of living to all of its citizens by 2111.

ANDRÉS BARBERO, A PARAGUAYAN POLYMATH *Ian Cameron Black and Robert Munro*

Andrés Barbero was a great philanthropist and benefactor. His life's work can still be seen in Paraguay today: the *Cruz Roja Paraguaya*, the *Museo Andrés Barbero*, the *Fundación La Piedad*, the *Sociedad Científica del Paraguay*, the *Academia de Historia* and the *Asociación Indigenista del Paraguay*, to name but a few. His main achievements are in three fields: medicine, education and indigenous studies, but his contribution goes far beyond these fields and touches almost every aspect of Paraguayan life from history, economics, agriculture, care of the elderly, guaraní language and more.

Andrew Barbero was born in Asunción on July 28th, 1877, the only male child of Italian parents. He graduated from high school and was immediately appointed to teach physics. At the same time he undertook the installation of an x-ray laboratory — the first in Paraguay — and a wireless telegraph. In 1898 he graduated top of the class as a pharmacist and went on to study medicine. As a medical student he gave lectures in physics, botany, histology, physiology and embryology. He was among the first to receive a medical doctorate in Paraguay in 1904, and so highly was he regarded that in 1905 he was appointed Director of the National Vaccine Laboratory and curator of the Natural History Museum of the *Colegio Nacional de la Capital*. In 1908 at the age of 31 he became Dean of the Faculty of Medicine.

In addition to his university responsibilities, the government nominated him a member of the National Education Council and of the National Health Council, of which he became Director in 1917. He promoted an active campaign against tropical diseases and under his direction some 22 commissions were set up to study and made recommendation on how to fight malaria and other sicknesses then endemic in Paraguay. In 1908 he made the first of his three visits to Europe, where he was delegated by the government to gather ideas for the creation in Paraguay of the national institute for technical and industrial training. At the same time he took an interest in agricultural production and nutrition in rural areas. He served a term as president of the *Consejo de Agricultura e Industria* from where he encouraged the cultivation of wheat, and later became a member of the board of the *Banco Agrícola*.

His chief concern was public health. As Director of the *Departamento Nacional de Higiene* he promoted a vigorous campaign throughout the country that resulted in 1500 wells for clean drinking water and the construction of over 37000 hygienic lavatories in rural communities. He also oversaw the placement of medical doctors throughout the country and established clinics specialising in various diseases including TB and mother-and-baby units. He oversaw the construction of a modern surgical unit at the *Hospital de Clínicas* in Asunción (known today as *Sala V*) and he lead the fight against the flu epidemic of 1918 and the following year he was involved in establishing the *Liga Nacional contra la Tuberculosis* and was its president for many years.

In 1919 upon his return from Europe, Dr. Barbero promoted the creation of the *Cruz Roja Paraguaya*, (Paraguayan Red Cross) of which he became the chief benefactor. He funded and supervised the construction of a modern building in Asunción to house among other facilities, a large maternity unit and the first nursing school in Paraguay.

On September 20th 1926 the Red Cross went to the aid of the city of Encarnación after a severe hurricane, an unusual event in Paraguay, completely destroyed the *Villa Baja* of this city in the south of the country.

The government of Paraguay nominated Dr. Barbero to numerous public offices. In 1920 he was appointed Mayor of Asunción, in 1933 Minister of Economic Affairs and in 1937 Chairman of the National Commission for Works and Development. He was also behind the foundation of the National Cancer Institute — which today bears the name of his sisters Maria and Josefa — and he endowed an old folk's home and its adjacent fine chapel in the crypt of which are to be found the Barbero family tombs.

In 1942, in recognition of his work in the fields of medicine, professional education, ethnology and support for the needy, the government of Paraguay awarded Dr. Barbero the National Order of Merit with the grade of Commander. He also received numerous decoration from other governments.

His life's work always had a social purpose: he was a great humanitarian. But his work did not cease with his death in 1951. His sisters, Maria and Josefa, together with his brother-in-law, Luis Viola, used his estate to endow a charitable foundation in his memory: *Fundación La Piedad* which seeks to perpetuate Dr. Barbero's memory and ideals by continuing to promote and support numerous initiatives in t he fields of science, education and culture.

The Andrés Barbero Museum in Asunción and the polymath himself (inset). His doctoral certificate, the first in Paraguay, carries 'No. 1' and can be seen at the museum.

Paraguay is hurtling towards the bicentenary of its independence. Spurred by booming commercial agriculture, the growth rate has ratcheted up during the first decade of the new millennium and the 9% forecast for 2010 is the highest in 29 years. Paraguay is now the fourth largest exporter of soybean in the world and the eighth largest beef exporter. This faster growth is producing a dramatic transformation of the urban landscape. The hitherto sleepy towns in the Asunción metropolitan area are becoming vibrant cities in their own right, while in the east flourishing new urban centres have emerged at Santa Rita and Salto del Guairá to challenge the hitherto dominance of Ciudad del Este.

The rapid spread of mobile telephones and motorcycles have become emblematic of this faster growth. Paraguay now has over seven million mobile lines in operation, an average of more than one for every person in the country. In rural areas, motorcycles that are imported and assembled in Paraguay are spreading like wildfire and have become the new status symbol for youth in villages and towns alike. The IT revolution has been slow to hit Paraguay because of the inadequacy of the infrastructure network, but as the fibre optic cable network spreads, the Ministry of Education has ambitious plans to extend a pilot project in Caacupé and provide free laptops to all school children.

EPILOGUE

In addition to the spread of hypermarkets, luxury shopping centres have opened on the northern edge of Asunción catering for the high-income earners. For the first time in the history of the country the state has begun to introduce the foundations of an embryonic welfare state. Monthly conditional cash transfers ($60) are now being paid to around 120,000 of the poorest families in neglected departments such as San Pedro and Caazapá. An old age pension ($76 per month) is also being rolled out — initially to 5,000 low-income dwellers of the Bañados slum area that skirts the bay of Asunción. Consultation fees have been abolished in all state medical facilities.

Major new infrastructure projects are getting off the ground.
The Asunción Bay Highway Project, first mooted in the 1960s and on which construction began in mid-2010, will revitalise the run-down historic port area and provide the first rapid transit system to the city centre as well as relocating low-income bay dwellers whose homes had been flooded every few years. New high voltage electricity transmission lines are being constructed from the Itaipú and Yacyretá hydro plants that will put an end to Asunción's summer blackouts and boost the country's industrial potential. The historic triangular highway network linking Asunción, Ciudad del Este and Encarnación is being extended as a new north-south arterial route emerges linking Pedro Juan Caballero to Encarnación.

The global image of Paraguay is also changing and, in the process, the tired stereotype of a 'forgotten' country comprising only military dictators, Nazis and steam trains is being rapidly discarded. Indeed Paraguay is now no longer off the map. Success at the 2010 Football World Cup, where Paraguay reached the quarter-final round for the first time, while giving a psychological boost to the people, has also made a significant contribution to the country's image as a major footballing nation. In fact, the 'Albirrojas' have now reached the last four consecutive World Cup finals and in three of these were defeated by teams that went on to reach the final — France (1998), Germany (2006) and Spain (2010) - and in two cases (France and Spain) were the overall winner. The growing global recognition of Agustín Barrios as a leading composer for the classical guitar, the world tours of guitarist Berta Rojas, the performances around the world of Luís Szarán's youth orchestra, *Sonidos de la Tierra*, as well as the flourishing talent of a new generation of Paraguayan harpists, are all also contributing to the image of the country endowed with musical excellence. The rich fauna and flora of the country are also attracting more international attention as new niche tourist markets develop in bird-watching and Chaco safaris as well as tours of Paraguay's heritage of Jesuit *reducciones*.

Of course, problems still remain and Paraguay faces enormous challenges as it enters its third century: education, job creation, income inequality and rampant deforestation of the Chaco. However, Paraguay has the potential to become a great prosperous and progressive nation. Natural resources are abundant, the land is fertile and the climate benign. Much is being done in order to provide an improved and sustainable lifestyle to its near seven million inhabitants. The peaceful transition to democracy, in 1993, followed, in 2008, by closely contested elections and coalition politics are landmarks to be celebrated.

Building on its strong sense of national identity (*ñande reko*), and a sense of common purpose (*oñondivepa*), then, as they say in Paraguay, "*enteromba'e ikatu*" — all is possible.